THE SUNNY BORDER

Sun-Loving Perennials for Season-Long Color

By C. Colston Burrell

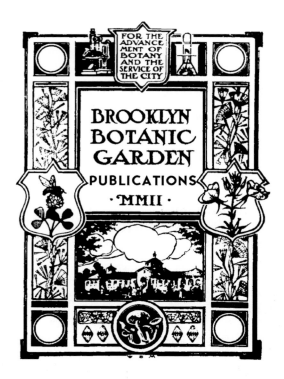

FOR THE ADVANCEMENT OF BOTANY AND THE SERVICE OF THE CITY

BROOKLYN BOTANIC GARDEN PUBLICATIONS · MMII ·

Janet Marinelli
SERIES EDITOR

Sigrun Wolff Saphire
SENIOR EDITOR

Mark Tebbitt
SCIENCE EDITOR

Leah Kalotay
ART DIRECTOR

Steven Clemants
VICE-PRESIDENT, SCIENCE & PUBLICATIONS

Judith D. Zuk
PRESIDENT

Elizabeth Scholtz
DIRECTOR EMERITUS

Handbook #172
Copyright © 2002 by Brooklyn Botanic Garden, Inc.
Handbooks in the *21st-Century Gardening Series,* formerly *Plants & Gardens,*
are published quarterly at 1000 Washington Ave., Brooklyn, NY 11225.
Subscription included in Brooklyn Botanic Garden subscriber membership dues ($35.00 per year).
ISBN # 1-889538-53-1
Printed by Science Press, a division of the Mack Printing Group.
Printed on recycled paper.

TABLE OF CONTENTS
The Sunny Border

INTRODUCTION:
The Sunny Border

A merica is addicted to perennials. Why? Pundits claim that perennial gardening is less work than replanting annuals every season and that perennials are more interesting than traditional low-maintenance shrubs and groundcovers. While this is true, I think the main reason is that people experience pleasure in tending a garden. Sure, we want low maintenance, but we enjoy the act of gardening, not just having a garden.

Design and planting are fun enough, but it's the daily or weekly interaction with my plants that I love. Discovering the emerging noses of the first daffodils during spring cleanup or expectantly checking the buds on a favorite peony make gardening so satisfying. Besides, most perennials have something interesting to offer in the way of foliage, flowers, or seed heads throughout the year, whereas annuals produce only blooms at their peak, after which they are yanked out and tossed.

For many, the perfect garden is a sun-drenched English perennial border, resplendent with masses of herbaceous plants in colorful sweeps. Yet not every gardener has a spot for such a grand display, or the time to maintain it. Fortunately, there are other ways to enjoy the beautiful array of plants that thrive with a full day of sunshine. A sunny border can consist of a purely wild planting of prairie or meadow wildflowers and grasses, for example, or an informal mixture of old-fashioned cottage-garden favorites.

What's more, herbaceous perennials need not be the only component of a sunny border. A well-designed perennial garden may also feature bulbs, grasses, ferns, and shrubs in what is called a mixed border. This allows you to layer

Filled with a riot of colors, shapes, and wonderful scents, a flower garden in bloom is a feast for all our senses, as well as a source of food and shelter for birds, insects, and other wildlife.

Colorful sweeps of blossoms, such as *Achillea* 'Moonshine' and 'Coronation Gold' and deep purple *Salvia nemorosa*, are the essence of a sunny border. Designs range from English-style perennial gardens to lovely plantings of native wildflowers and grasses.

plantings to great effect, the way nature layers its wild gardens. A garden with many vertical layers affords a high degree of aesthetic complexity and biological diversity, as well as structure and bloom throughout the season. Complexity and diversity are what make these gardens exciting.

To grow plants effectively, you must first understand the ground rules. "Growing Sun-Loving Plants" explores the environmental imperatives that shape the gardens we create and provides tips on how to transform nature's lessons into exciting and successful plantings. "Designing a Sunny Border" shows how to make the most of the colors, forms, and textures of perennials in stunning combinations that keep the garden in flower from spring through frost, as well as how to extend the season with foliage and decorative seed heads. "Planting and Maintenance" gives you step-by-step instructions on how to get your garden off the drawing board and into the ground.

Finally, the "Encyclopedia of Sun-Loving Perennials" covers more than 100 dramatic plants grouped by their soil-moisture preferences, from wet to dry, to help you create successful combinations of plants that share the same requirements. A list of nearly 100 flowering shrubs helps you layer your garden for season-long beauty. I hope that with this handbook as your guide, you will discover the many joys of gardens that celebrate the sun.

The typical turf-covered front yard can be transformed into a unique personal statement with a profusion of flowering perennials and shrubs.

A colorful planting of late-summer bloomers includes asters, goldenrods, black-eyed susans, and cardinal flowers.

GROWING SUN-LOVING PLANTS:
Lessons From Nature

T he more you know about the plants in your garden, the better you can accommodate their needs. The first step in knowing a plant is to find out where it grows in the wild. In nature, evolution has adapted plants to a variety of sun exposures and soil and moisture conditions. If a plant thrives in a particular spot in nature, it is likely to thrive under similar conditions in your garden.

Most of the plants we grow in our sunny borders evolved in grasslands, on rocky mountainsides, and in sunny marshes around the world. North America's prairies have given us such beautiful plants as blazing stars (*Liatris*), sunflowers (*Helianthus*), and milkweeds, including butterfly weed (*Asclepias tuberosa*). Yarrows (*Achillea*), calamints (*Calamintha*), and meadow sage (*Salvia nemorosa*) come from the meadows of Europe; peonies from southeastern Europe, the Caucasus, Siberia, Tibet, and China; balloon flowers (*Platycodon*) from wet meadows in Japan and eastern

Observe plants that thrive in wild habitats in your area to find out which types of plants will do well in your sunny garden.

Opposite: Bluebonnets and Indian paintbrush in a Texas meadow.

Right: Wetland plants growing in a California marsh.

AN EASY WAY TO IMPROVE YOUR SOIL

Almost any kind of soil can benefit from the addition of organic matter in the form of humus. Humus is decayed organic matter that is very fertile and has exceptional water-holding ability. Compost and well-composted manure are sources of humus.

An easy way to amend the soil is to add a layer of organic matter 4 to 6 inches deep over the entire planting bed. Incorporate it thoroughly to a depth of 10 to 12 inches. Break the soil up with a shovel or spading fork. Continue digging or spading until all large lumps of soil are broken up and the compost or manure is thoroughly mixed with the existing soil.

If the soil contains a large percentage of clay, add both organic matter and sand or fine gravel. Break the soil up as described above, then spread 2 inches each of compost and sharp builder's sand over the planting bed. Incorporate to a depth of 12 inches, mixing thoroughly with the soil.

Once all clods and clumps are broken up and the organic matter is thoroughly incorporated, smooth out the surface of the bed. Use a metal garden rake to even out any hills or dips. Remove any roots or other debris. Your site is now ready for planting.

A garden based on natural plant communities, such as this prairie, punctuated by Indian grass (*Sorghastrum nutans*), will be both beautiful and easy to maintain.

China; and Cape fuchsia (*Phygelius*) from stream banks in the mountains of southern Africa. The soils differ, the moisture levels are diverse, and the climates vary, but what each of these native plant communities have in common is an abundance of sunshine.

If you are new to gardening, observe which sun-loving plants thrive in your area by visiting nature preserves and other wild habitats. Notice, too, how nature combines these species into various plant associations or communities, from deserts and dry upland meadows to wet roadside ditches. Make these natural communities the foundation of your plant combinations, and your garden will be both beautiful and easy to maintain.

Degrees of Sunshine

Plants for a sunny border grow best with a minimum of 10 to 12 hours a day of direct sun in midsummer. The precise amount of sunshine required will vary, depending on the region and the particular plant. Not all plants are as adaptable as the ubiquitous daylily (*Hemerocallis* species) or border phlox (*Phlox paniculata*), which grow in nature in sunny woodland glades and in meadows. What's more, full sun in Minnesota is different from full sun in Mississippi. In Minnesota the sun is less intense, but in summer it stays light longer than in Mississippi. While balloon flower demands full sun in most gardens, in the deep South it will grow happily in partial shade. Success depends on choosing the best plants for your region. Check the Native Habitat heading in each plant entry in the "Encyclopedia of Sun-Loving Plants" (page 34) for information on where the species grows in the wild. If it is native to an area with a climate and growing conditions similar to yours, chances are the plant will do well for you.

Moisture Conditions

Native plant communities are classified by ecologists into three broad categories based on their moisture conditions: xeric or dry, hydric or wet, and mesic or moist. These moisture regimes are determined by both soil type and position in the landscape. In general, dry soils occur in upland areas or on sharply draining slopes. They are gravelly, sandy, or sandy loam soils. Hydric sites, including swales and other low spots where water collects, can be inundated during winter and spring. The soils in such areas tend to be heavy clays or highly organic peats. Mesic areas are seldom inundated by water, and the

Plants with silvery, waxy, fleshy, or small leaves are usually adapted to dry soils. The agave and succulents in the border at right require little water.

Different plants are adapted to different moisture conditions. Be sure to combine plants with similar moisture requirements. Gaura, Russian sage, daylilies, lavenders, and feather grass are all drought-tolerant.

soils typically are loams containing roughly equal portions of sand, silt, and clay. Rich, loamy soil is the kind gardeners traditionally have considered ideal, because they are neither too wet nor too dry for the most common garden plants.

Different plants are adapted to these various moisture conditions. Determine which type of soil you have and choose plants accordingly. Plants in the "Encyclopedia of Sun-Loving Plants" are organized according to their moisture preferences.

Dealing With Dry Soil

A perpetually dry spot may seem like an impossible challenge, but it can be transformed into a colorful oasis. Many popular perennials such as lavenders (*Lavandula*), purple coneflowers (*Echinacea*), yarrows (*Achillea*), yuccas, daylilies (*Hemerocallis*), and pinks (*Dianthus*) thrive in dry soil.

If your garden is high and sloping, with sandy or gravelly soil, or a sandy spot near the sea, water will quickly drain downhill or evaporate in the wind. The addition of organic matter will help the soil retain water. If the soil is solid clay, the addition of coarse sand or fine gravel, such as decomposed granite or chicken grit, along with organic matter will help keep the soil open so water soaks in rather than runs off. See "An Easy Way to Improve Your Soil" (page 10).

To succeed in gardening in such an environment, you need plants that will thrive under the existing conditions. In prairies, on sunny mountainsides, and on sand dunes, as well as in deserts, a wealth of beautiful plants grow that will thrive in a garden like yours.

Just by looking at a plant, experienced gardeners can get a pretty good idea of whether or not it is adapted to dry soils in full sun. The foliage is one key to where the plant thrives in nature. In areas where summers are hot, dry, or both, plants have small leaves, which are very efficient at producing food and lose relatively little moisture to transpiration. The more moisture a plant gets, the larger its leaves can be, but plants adapted to full sun seldom have leaves as large as those of shade-loving plants, such as hosta. If the leaves are waxy or fleshy, such as those of sedum, they are designed to hold water. Silvery or hairy leaves such as those of catmints (*Nepeta*) are also adapted to dry, sunny areas because the hairs reflect light and act like insulation, keeping the plant from overheating and wilting.

Another way plants cope with sun is to store moisture in their roots or stems. If a plant grows from a bulb, corm, tuber, or tuberous root, chances are it is sun- and drought-tolerant. Perennials with deep taproots are also good choices. Think of tap-rooted false indigo (*Baptisia australis*) on a dry roadside or the thick rhizome of a bearded iris, designed to survive the long, dry Mediterranean summer.

Mulch is a great help in conserving moisture on dry soils. Choose a porous mulch so that water will quickly filter through and enter the soil

Moisture-loving plants, such as lobelias and sweet flag, are well suited for wet spots.

Big bluestem grass and prairie coneflower are two North American plants well adapted to the growing conditions in midwestern prairies, where they are native.

rather than run off. Don't add too much, though, as plants adapted to dry conditions are easily smothered and will rot if they're covered with soggy mulch. About one inch of composted bark or shredded leaves is sufficient.

Making the Most of Moisture

If you have a low sunny spot that does not drain well, a soggy streamside or a pond, you can grow plants that demand constant moisture. Wet soil allows you to grow a variety of bold, beautiful plants—like queen-of-the-prairie (*Filipendula rubra*)—that will not otherwise thrive in most gardens. Astilbes and ligularias also thrive in sun if their feet are wet. Hydric gardens are lush and colorful, and many moisture-loving plants like cardinal flower (*Lobelia cardinalis*) and joe-pye weed (*Eupatorium*) are magnets for butterflies.

Naturally wet soil is often high in organic matter and very fertile. A low spot in your yard may be wet because a clay hardpan is keeping moisture from draining away. If the soggy spot is solid clay, adding some organic matter like compost will help your garden grow. Digging in mucky soil is difficult, so choose a dry spell to do soil preparation. If the spot is always wet, spread a 10- to 12-inch layer of compost over the existing soil, and plant right into the compost.

Plant Layers

Native plant communities are arranged in layers to create a complex but seamless whole. Layers in a forest are easy to see, from the tallest trees down to the ferns and tiny mosses on the forest floor. Grasslands and other sunny plant communities are also layered. Small wildflowers and native bulbs bloom early and are topped by later-blooming wildflowers and grasses, which form the highest layer unless shrubs are present. Look at nature's layering and use these vertical patterns to add harmony and complexity to your garden.

Sunny Borders for Every Region

THE NORTHEAST

In this region, bedrock is close to the surface, and soils are generally thin and highly acidic. The gardening season is short, except near the coast, with USDA hardiness zones ranging from 3 to 7. This means gardening can be a challenge, especially in the more northern areas. The advantages of gardening in northern latitudes or at higher elevations in mountainous regions are low humidity and delightfully cool summer days. Cool temperatures mean that moisture evaporates slowly, so supplemental watering is only necessary during extended dry spells. Plants grow more slowly when temperatures are cool, producing stronger, less succulent stems. Strong growth is more resistant to damage from insects and diseases. Towering delphiniums and hollyhocks (*Alcea* species), huge fragrant peonies, glorious asters, and disease-free roses are the pride of northern gardeners, as are the fiery leaves of maples in autumn.

THE MID-ATLANTIC

By and large, eastern North America is dominated by deciduous forests, but meadows and old fields (mixtures of grasses, perennials, and shrubs), ablaze with color in summer, are found in breaks in the forest and on sandy coastal plains.

Gardeners need to choose heat- and disease-resistant perennials that tolerate the high temperatures and humidity of a mid-Atlantic summer, but in general they are fortunate, as plants thrive thanks to mild winters and long, balmy autumns. This area covers Zones 5 to 7, depending on altitude and distance from the ocean. Soils are mostly clay loams or sandy loams, and though fertile, they usually need organic matter to increase moisture retention. In this temperate region, many perennials from both north and south can be grown successfully together, making exciting gardens that are colorful from late winter until October or November.

THE SOUTHEAST

The Southeast is characterized by sandy plains near the coast, with richer and moister clay-based soils farther inland. Though clay retains moisture, it may shrink and crack as it dries, breaking brittle roots. Gardeners in this area need to add large quantities of organic matter to the soil and use mulch to retain moisture.

In summer, plants must endure soaring daytime temperatures, sultry humidity, and nights that often feel no cooler than the daytime. Fungal and bacterial diseases can be a real problem; choose resistant varieties when possible and space plants properly to encourage healthy air circulation.

Native plant communities are arranged in layers to create a complex but seamless whole. Imitate nature by integrating shrubs, such as the flowering dogwood, above, into your perennial border.

However, late winter and spring are glorious, with colorful bulbs and flowering shrubs, and the long fall is full of blooming salvias and asters.

In Zones 7 to 9, native meadow flowers as well as old-fashioned pass-along plants like scarlet rose mallow (*Hibiscus coccineus*) have been grown for generations. Many tropical plants, such as cannas and bananas (*Musa* species), can be overwintered in the ground here, making stunning gardens when mixed with more traditional perennials.

THE MIDWEST AND PLAINS STATES

The vast region between the Appalachian range and the Rocky Mountains was once dominated by prairies. The easternmost portion of the prairie province has deep, rich soils and ample rainfall, making for luxuriant gardens. As you move west, precipitation decreases. Areas that lie in the rain shadow of the Rockies receive less than 16 inches of rain per year, so garden plants there must be chosen carefully.

The intense winter cold (Zones 3 to 5), summer heat, and periodic drought in the region produce stressful conditions for plants. The good news is that winter snows protect plants from the worst of the cold. Preparing the soil well and choosing regionally native or adapted species with exceptional hardiness are mandatory for success, especially where the soil is thin and dry. A protective mulch of chopped leaves can help the garden through the winter, and it's imperative in areas where you cannot count on consistent snow cover.

THE SOUTHWEST AND SOUTHERN CALIFORNIA

The mild summer and winter temperatures of the Southwest and southern California make it possible to grow a variety of plants from various regions. Days are sunny and dry, and nights are cool. Most of the rain falls in winter, leaving a long season of little or no rainfall. Plants must be able to endure drought.

Many traditional perennial garden plants do poorly here despite the cool summers because the winters are not cold enough to satisfy their dormancy requirements. Native plants such as beard tongue (*Penstemon*) and yucca, as well as those from Mediterranean climates, such as catmints, sages (*Salvia* species), and lavenders, perform best. Succulents and cacti are good choices for the sunny border, as are woolly-leafed plants that may rot in wetter areas of the country.

THE PACIFIC NORTHWEST

Gardeners in this large region encompassing Zones 6 to 8 generally enjoy cool summers, ideal for growing perennials. Coastal areas have mild winters as well, making them a gardening paradise—the perfection so admired in English gardening books is most attainable here. Autumn, winter, and spring are the seasons with the highest rainfall.

The northern Pacific coast receives 50 to 100 inches of rain a year, giving rise to a lush and productive temperate rainforest. Clay-based soils are usually shallow and acidic, so good soil preparation may be necessary. Mountainous regions are colder but offer wonderful possibilities for gardening with hardy, drought-tolerant plants.

Designing a Sunny Border

Asuccessful sunny border design that emulates nature begins with dreams, is guided by a clear vision, and is recorded in a plan. At the start, indulge yourself in the luxury of dreaming. Then turn your garden dream into a reality guided by a design. Great gardens can be made without a plan, but for most people, it is an important starting point. It helps you visualize what is in your mind's eye.

Locating the Garden

Begin with the selection of a site. Where you place the sunny border determines what you can grow. Choose a location suited to the overall layout of your yard. Think in practical as well as aesthetic terms. Where is the water spigot? Where do the kids play? Place your garden out of harm's way. Consider views from the house, the border's relationship to the terrace or deck, and its proximity to other landscape features. The garden will look its best if the components are integrated into a unified whole. One large bed often looks nicer and is easier to maintain than several smaller ones.

Carefully assess the size and style of your flower bed. Let existing features, such as the shape of the lawn or the terrace around which you plan to install the bed, guide your design. If you have never delineated an outdoor space or given a pleasing shape to your lawn, start there, and then add the flower bed or borders to complement the space. Don't skimp on the size of your border: You need ample space to accommodate a variety of plants for a long season of blooms. Make room for 30 to 40 plants at a minimum. And

Turn the garden of your dreams into a reality. To create a design that suits the site, take your time to determine the style and layout of your flower bed.

Consider access to your garden as you develop your design plan. You need to be able to reach all plants from the edges or from internal paths. If you have to step into the flower bed to take care of a plant, you will compact the soil.

remember, the farther the garden is from your viewing point, the larger it must be to make an impact.

Consider access to the garden as you develop your plan. You need to be able to reach all areas of the garden from the edges or from internal paths. A person of average height can reach about 2½ feet into a bed. A border that's accessible from one side should be no more than three to four feet deep; if it's wider, it needs a rear or central path. A bed that's accessible from all sides can be up to five or six feet deep without a path. If you'd like to arrange flowers in front of a backdrop of shrubs, create a bed that's at least six to eight feet deep. If you have room, 12 feet is ideal.

Creating a Base Map

The easiest way to design your garden is by drawing up a plan. You will need a few tools to get started: a ruler, graph paper, a pencil, and a tape measure. The first step is to decide on the scale for your drawing. A common scale is one square on the graph paper to two square feet of garden space. If you are planning a large garden, one square per three feet may work better. Tape a large sheet of graph paper to a table. Record on the paper the corners of the house, property lines, and other existing features that will act as reference points. Then spread a piece of tracing paper over your base map. Sketch the shape and size of your future garden area on the tracing paper. Now you are ready to begin designing.

Combining the Plants

Choosing plants is my favorite part of designing a garden. Start by reading the plant descriptions in the "Encyclopedia of Sun-Loving Perennials" (page 34), keeping in mind soil and moisture conditions. Make a list or chart of the plants that appeal to you, jotting down flower color, bloom time, height, and spread of every plant. Once completed, your list will be useful throughout the design process.

First, choose a few outstanding anchor plants that bloom in different seasons. These plants will become the centerpieces for a series of plant combinations. Next pick complementary plants that bloom at the same time as the anchor plants. Consider flower color and size, the form of the plant, and the texture of the leaves.

Draw the plants or cut pictures from magazines and make a collage. Place rounded forms

Top and bottom: Combine plants to highlight their individual attributes, pairing rounded forms with spiky ones, setting airy shapes against bold ones.

To maximize the visual appeal of your garden, group together the flowering plants that bloom at the same time. Above, top, is Mediterranean spurge (*Euphorbia characias*).

next to spiky ones and use sprawling plants, such as verbena and winecups (*Callirhoe*) to weave together larger clumps and unify the front edge of the bed. Don't place too many similar shapes together. Place the tallest plants in the middle or back unless they are airy enough to be transparent, like meadow rues (*Thalictrum*).

The secret to successful design lies in choosing and combining plants to maximize their individual attributes. If you know the characteristics of the plants, you can layer them to get the most bloom in the smallest space. You can arrange plants so that combinations of spring bloomers are topped in summer and again in fall by new combinations of flowers. Use one plant to show off another or to fill a space left when one goes dormant. Contrast billowing, airy plants with bolder textures. To maximize the visual appeal of your garden, concentrate the flowers that bloom at the same time. Keep linking pleasing, varied plant combinations until you have filled your garden space. Be sure to repeat one plant, key color, or strong form throughout the garden to maintain unity and create rhythm. A unified design is essential to make the garden look and feel right.

Shrubs are natural additions to flower gardens. From earliest spring through the hard frosts of fall, shrubs enhance the landscape with a kaleidoscope of flowers, foliage, and fruits. In winter, bare twigs or evergreen foliage add texture to a barren or snowy landscape. In early spring the branches provide a framework for the garden and a background for early flowers and bulbs. In autumn, foliage and fruit steal the show from fading asters and other flowers.

Laying Out the Bed

Once you are happy with your plan and have the plants lined up, prepare the planting bed by amending the soil and raking the surface smooth. Using a tape measure, wooden stakes, and string, mark off one-, two-, or three-foot grid intervals, depending on the size of the garden and the intricacy of the design. Measure out squares and spray the outline of the grid on the soil with bio-safe florist's paint, or trace the grid in the soil with a rake handle or other tool. Lay out the entire grid first. Now you are ready to set out the plants according to the plan, referring to the grid to get the spacing right. If you measure the length of your trowel, you can use it as a handy tool for fine-tuning. I prefer to lay out the entire garden before I plant. I usually need to make adjustments, and I might change my mind when I see actual plant combinations in place.

I view a garden as a work in progress. Whether it is two months, two years, or two decades old, there is inevitably room for improvement as the design matures. The best design tool you have is your shovel. The wonderful thing about plants is that you can move them. Planting and tending a garden is a creative process. Your efforts will be paid back tenfold as you eagerly await the opening of the first daffodil, breathe the intoxicating fragrance of a mock orange, and revel in the beauty of a summer border ablaze with glowing colors.

Planting and Maintenance

All gardens require care. I think of gardening as entertainment, not work. Sure, some of the tasks are labor-intensive, but it is the planting and tending of the garden that teach me about nature and natural processes. I enter this relationship from a sense of wonder rather than a sense of duty. Working with nature, instead of against it, is the route to low maintenance and natural harmony. The way to get there is through organic methods and proper planting.

Buying Plants

Once you have sized up your site, created a good design, and compiled a list of plants, it's time to go shopping and plant your garden. Retail nurseries and garden centers are great places to look for plants. Unless you are seeking a rarity or a brand-new introduction, a garden center should have everything you need. The perennials you find there are grown in containers—neat, well established, and easy to carry away.

Mail-order nurseries are another source of great plants, and they may be the only way to find a particular cultivar, an unusual species or a good selection of native perennials. Order early to assure the best selection, and be sure to specify a ship date that's appropriate to your area. Unpack the plants as soon as they arrive. Water containerized plants well. Many mail-order plants are shipped bare-root. Inspect the roots for signs of damage. If the roots are dry, soak them in warm water for several hours before you plant. If they are rotting, cut off the affected portions. Keep the plants cool and shaded until you can plant them. If you cannot get them in the ground right away, pot them up.

Keep your garden attractive through the winter by leaving decorative foliage and seed heads in place when you clean up in fall.

Meadow and prairie gardens are often planted with plugs or seed. Plugs are seedlings or young plants grown in the type of cell packs most often used for annuals. Plugs are inexpensive, easy to plant, and quick to establish. Seeds are an even cheaper option. Many wildflower specialists offer seed mixes prepared for your location, soil, and moisture conditions. Make sure the plants are native. Some wildflower mixes are mostly composed of non-native annuals. Some nurseries will create custom mixes for you, or you can create your own if you know which plants you wish to grow. When seeds arrive, store them in the refrigerator until you're ready to sow them.

Planting Techniques

Provided the soil is well prepared, installing containerized plants is easy. Remove the plant from the container by inverting it with your hand cupped around the plant's crown. Shake the container or rap the rim on a solid surface to dislodge the plant. Right the plant once it falls into your hand, shake most of the soil off the roots, and disentan-

Top left: Soak bare-root plants in warm water before planting.

Bottom left: Remove a containerized plant from its pot, shake most of the soil off the roots and disentangle them.

Top right: Trim off excess roots of a pot-bound plant.

Bottom right: Use a shovel to divide large plants.

gle them. Examine the roots to see if the plant is pot-bound, and cut any tight, circling, or badly bent and twisted roots with sharp shears. It's important to take care of the roots at this point; otherwise the plant may not get established properly.

Dig a hole twice as wide as the longest roots. If this is unreasonable, trim the roots to a manageable length. Depending on the size of the plant, the hole needs to be three to five inches deep. Make a cone of soil in the center of the hole tall enough to bring the crown of the plant level with the soil surface. Spread the roots evenly over the mound. Holding the crown in place, fill in with soil to bring the hole up to grade. Firm around the crown, level the soil, and water the plants well. Never let the soil dry out during the first growing season.

Bare-root plants are just that: plants without soil covering the roots. They must be planted in the garden or potted up as soon as they arrive. Installing a bare-root plant is easy, because you do not have to break up the root ball as you do with containerized stock. Dig a hole in a well-prepared bed, and plant as above.

Like bare-root plants, plugs are easier to plant in well-prepared soil, but they can also be successfully planted in unprepared soil. Remove the plug from its cell by pushing the root ball up from the bottom. If the roots are tangled use sharp shears or your fingers to pull them apart.

Dig a small hole and set the plug against the back of the hole, with the crown level with the existing soil. Fill in around the roots and firm the soil to hold the plug in place. Water plants well and keep them moist until the new root system is established.

Proper Spacing

In a garden that basks in full sun, each plant can develop to its full height and spread. The prettiest gardens are those in which all plants are given ample room to spread without being so far apart that gaps appear in the garden. In a perfectly planted, mature garden, full, rounded crowns slightly overlap each other, leaving no blank spaces, which is a good thing, as open space is an invitation for weeds to grow. To keep maintenance to a minimum, you need to get the spacing right.

Every plant has a predictable height and spread, giving you a good idea of optimum spacing in the garden. One of the most common mistakes is to place plants too close together in a new bed. By the time the plants have been in the ground for a year or so, they are so entangled that you cannot appreciate the forms and flowers of the individual plants. What's worse, they do not get adequate light or air circulation, and they may become weakened or diseased.

How do you determine the optimum spacing for each plant? Check the "Encyclopedia of Sun-Loving Perennials" (page 34) to learn the average height and spread of the plants you want to grow. The tags on nursery-bought plants also provide this information; they may even tell you how far apart to space each plant. Use this as a guide, but do not follow the recommendations slavishly. Some plants, especially upright and spiky ones such as irises and delphiniums, can be placed close together in clumps or drifts. Plants like oriental poppies (*Papaver orientale*) fill a large space when in bloom but disappear after flowering, so adjacent plants should be placed close by to fill the gap left when the poppies go dormant.

Watering

During the first year, watering is mandatory for new plants just getting established in your border. In summer the entire garden may need extra moisture. Soaker hoses are the best way to get water into the soil with minimal loss to evaporation. Loop soaker hoses through beds, spacing the loops according to the manufacturer's suggestions. Once the hoses are in place, disguise them with an attractive and water-conserving mulch. On average, moist- and wet-soil gardens need an inch of water a week. Plants adapted to dry conditions can get by with less. If rain is insufficient, turn on the hoses.

Applying a layer of mulch on your flower beds has many advantages. It helps suppress weeds, insulates the soil from summer heat and winter cold, and conserves moisture.

The manufacturer's directions will tell you how long it takes to deliver the equivalent of one inch of rain.

Sprinklers are another option, though they are wasteful. Place them carefully, so you don't waste water showering driveways or other impervious surfaces. Water for two to four hours once a week, rather than for frequent, short spells. To reduce loss to evaporation, water in the morning or in the evening.

Mulching

Mulches keep beds looking tidy and help suppress weeds while insulating the soil from heat and conserving moisture. Think regionally when you choose a mulch: Local materials are less expensive because they are produced nearby, and they blend more naturally with the garden.

Well-composted organic mulches are best. Chopped leaves make an excellent fine-textured mulch. Horse, sheep, and cow manures are also good. Be sure to use only aged manure, though, as anything fresh from the barn will burn plants. Manure is usually mixed with some kind of bedding, such as sawdust, wood chips, or straw. If you can find a supplier of shredded manure, all the better. Shredding grinds up the bedding and blends it together, making a fine- to medium-textured mulch that is attractive and easy to apply. In addition to insulating the soil, these products slowly release nitrogen.

Different types of mulches are prevalent in different areas of the country. In the Southeast and the Pacific Northwest, pine bark is available as a by-product of the lumber industry. Choose the finest grade of bark—preferably aged three years—when selecting mulch for a herbaceous border. Large bark chips are appropriate for shrubs and trees.

In the arid West, rock mulches may be appropriate in some situations. Fine-textured rock from local sources blends seamlessly with the native stone so prominent in these regions and is a great soil insulator. In the East, rock mulches usually look out of place.

As a general rule, the heavier the mulch, the more thinly it should be applied. For most mulches, a one- to two-inch layer spread evenly over the garden in early spring is ideal. Airy materials like chopped leaves can be distributed a little thicker, as they will settle. Use rock mulches sparingly, usually about one inch deep. Apply the chosen mulch after you have removed spent stems and tidied the garden.

Staking

Tall plants have a tendency to flop when exposed to strong wind and rain. Humus-rich, loamy soils often exacerbate the situation, as they provide a rich diet that promotes fast, succulent growth. To avoid the distress and disarray of toppled spikes and peonies with their faces in the mud, proper staking is essential. Tall, narrow spikes like those of blazing stars (*Liatris*) can be individually attached to slender stakes stuck in the ground alongside the stems. Full-crowned plants like peonies are best grown through hoops, placed over the clumps as they emerge from the ground. Most of the plants discussed in this book do not need staking if they are grown in the soil and moisture conditions they prefer.

Weeding

Weeds rob nutrients, moisture, and light from your plants. Keeping weeds down is imperative to a healthy, attractive garden. Weeds are most abundant in a new garden. If you stay on top of weeding in the first few years, you will have an easier time as the garden matures and fills in. There is little space for weeds in a fully planted garden, where mature plants shade the soil and keep weed seeds from germinating. Tree seedlings and some persistent perennial weeds like dandelions may require monthly patrols and removal. Dislodge large tap-rooted weeds with an asparagus fork or trowel to ensure that they will not resprout.

Cutting Back

Plants like catmints (*Nepeta*) and hardy geraniums produce mounds of growth covered with blooms in early summer. After the flowers fade you can cut the tangle of stems back to keep the clump neat and in scale. Cut the stems back by two thirds, or cut them to the ground if the plants have basal leaves, such as hardy geraniums and lady's mantle (*Alchemilla mollis*). Often, this shearing will promote fresh growth and renewed flowering.

Throughout the summer, as flowers fade and growth declines, cut back plants that look bedraggled. Remove most spent flower stalks, but leave some to allow attractive seed heads to form. At the end of the season, prepare the garden for winter. After frost, cut back all succulent plants like daylilies (*Hemerocallis* species), peonies, and irises to where the new foliage is visible

just above the ground. Plants such as phlox and salvias die to the ground, so cut them down. I like to leave decorative seed heads like those of false indigo (*Baptisia australis*) and rose mallow (*Hibiscus moscheutos*) for winter interest. After the ground freezes, mulch the beds with chopped leaves or another light mulch to protect the crowns from winter burn. In early spring, cut down any plants left standing to make room for the new season's growth.

After the flowers fade, cut back spent blooms. In many plants, such as the *Artemisia* at right, this promotes fresh growth and leads to renewed flowering a few weeks later.

Pick plants suited to the growing conditions in your garden to keep diseases and insect pests at bay. Above: powdery mildew on garden phlox. Inset: aphids on bleeding heart.

Dividing and Transplanting

Sooner or later, many of your herbaceous plants are going to outgrow their allotted space and need to be divided. Lift the plants in early spring or as they are going dormant in fall. Shake excess soil from the roots, so you can see what you are doing. If the plants have discrete crowns, pull or cut these apart. If you are dividing a running plant like bee balm or yarrow, break off the vigorous portions around the outside of the clump and discard the spent woody center. Use a shovel or spade to divide large plants such as daylilies and ornamental grasses. Chop the clumps into smaller sections and replant the divided clumps into soil that has been enriched with compost.

You may find seedlings popping up that are perfect candidates for transplanting. Your goal is to disturb the plants as little as possible, so move them in early spring before the plants are in full growth or in autumn when they are going dormant. Insert your shovel or trowel all around the plant, loosen the soil, and lift the freed root ball out intact. Replant it in a hole of the same proportions, and move the excess soil to the original hole.

Pests and Diseases

One of the most important things you can do to keep pests and diseases at bay is to choose plants wisely, making sure to pick species that are suited to the growing conditions in your garden. Fortunately, if you match the plants to the site, install them properly, and give them the care they need, you will have few problems. The practices that lead to the overall health of your garden and its many denizens—frequent application of compost, proper pruning, wise watering, and good sanitation, among others—can suppress most plant maladies.

Insects are the most common form of life on earth. To a greater or lesser extent, the best strategy is to live with the minor damage they cause in your garden. When the garden is in balance, beneficial and predatory insects and other insect-eating animals, such as birds and bats, keep most pest species in check. If things get out of balance and a pest invades or a disease breaks out, refer to reliable sources, such as Brooklyn Botanic Garden handbooks *Natural Insect Control* and *Natural Disease Control* for the least-toxic treatment options.

Growing With the Sunny Border

As your garden grows and matures, it will take on a lush look that unifies the design. You will not be able to freeze the garden in time, however. As conditions change in the garden, the composition will also change. Plants will grow too large and will need division. Seedlings will come up in the oddest places. Aging shrubs will produce more shade, and some plants will die out. The processes of nature are always at work. Enjoy and utilize the opportunities they provide.

Encyclopedia
of Sun-Loving Perennials

P lants in this encyclopedia are divided by soil preference for easy reference. Each entry includes a description of the plant, tips on how to grow and maintain it, and recommendations on how to combine it with other plants to achieve spectacular effects. Related species with ornamental value are also noted.

Invasive Plants

Some popular garden plants have escaped into natural areas, where they spread rampantly and threaten native plant habitats. To check whether a plant you want to grow in your garden may be problematic, visit the "Pest Alerts" section of Brooklyn Botanic Garden's web site at www.bbg.org/gar2/pestalerts/, which includes links to the invasive plant council in your area and various local, national, and international databases of invasive species.

The flowers of fern-leaf yarrow dry to an attractive mustard-yellow as they age.

Perennials for Dry Areas

Achillea filipendulina
FERN-LEAF YARROW

NATIVE HABITAT Open meadows and damp swales of the Caucasus and Central Asia

HARDINESS ZONES 3 to 9

Fern-leaf yarrow brings the brilliant light of the sun to the summer garden. Dozens of 3- to 4-foot erect stems sport dense flat heads of small, frilly flowers with staying power. Plants bloom for a month or more, and the heads dry to mustard-yellow as they age, keeping the show running all summer. And they will rebloom if deadheaded. Aromatic, deeply incised, ferny olive-green leaves give the fibrous-rooted plant, which spreads to 3 feet wide, its common name.

HOW TO GROW Plant fern-leaf yarrow in average, dry to moist, well-drained soil in full sun or light shade. Yarrows are tough, easy-care perennials. Rich soils promote luxuriant growth and weak stems. Plants spread rapidly and need frequent division. Lift clumps every three years in early spring or fall. Replant vigorous portions into amended soil. Plants are prone to powdery mildew, a cottony white coating on the leaves, especially in areas with warm, humid nights.

RELATED SPECIES *Achillea* 'Coronation Gold' grows 3 feet tall with stout self-supporting stems, gray-green leaves, and 5-inch-wide clusters of bright mustard-yellow flowers. Zones 3 to 9. The Galaxy Series has 2- to 3-inch flower heads on sturdy stems. The flowers fade as they age, giving the plants a multicolored appearance. Plants grow 1 to $2^{1}/_{2}$ feet tall and wide. Zones 3 to 8. *A.* × 'Moonshine' is a popular hybrid reaching 1 to 2 feet tall, with blue-gray foliage and sulphur-yellow flowers that are excellent for cutting. Zones 3 to 7.

COMPANION PLANTS Yarrows are mainstays for drought-prone gardens. Place them at the front or middle of formal perennial borders with blue-flowered catmints (*Nepeta*) and purple salvias for contrast. Create a color harmony with red-eyed yellow daylilies (*Hemerocallis*) and golden-leafed *Spiraea thunbergii* 'Ogon'. In meadows and other informal gardens, combine them with grasses and wildflowers.

Anthemis tinctoria
GOLDEN MARGUERITE

NATIVE HABITAT Steppes, roadsides, and waste places throughout Europe

HARDINESS ZONES 3 to 7

This floriferous perennial lights up summer borders with perfect lemon-yellow daisies sporting large, button-like centers. The rich green leaves look like curly parsley, sparsely clothing the lax stems that reach 2 to 3½ feet. Plants tend to flop, even in lean soils, creating an informal clump several feet wide. Some selections have creamy yellow flowers with darker centers.

HOW TO GROW Well-drained nearly neutral sandy soil suits golden marguerite best. Plants tolerate alka-line, high-calcium soils. Rich soil promotes gluttony and a short life span. Stake plants if their lax posture offends you. To promote bushy growth and good air circulation and to prevent stem rot, especially where humidity is high, cut the plants back hard after flowering, leaving 2 to 5 inches of stem. Divide plants every two to three years after flowering to keep them vigorous. This plant does best in the northern half of the country where summers are seldom hot and steamy.

RELATED SPECIES *Anthemis sanctijohannis* is similar in size and habit but features brilliant orange-yellow flowers. Zones 3 to 7.

COMPANION PLANTS The bright yellow flowers add zest to hot-color borders with blanket flowers (*Gaillardia*), sundrops (*Oenothera*), orange or red daylilies (*Hemerocallis*), and deep purple salvias. Pale cultivars complement pastel color schemes of geraniums, lavenders, irises, and coneflowers (*Echinacea*). The flowers light up the garden in evening as they catch the glow of the summer moon.

Golden marguerites tend to flop, creating a large informal clump.

The aromatic silver foliage of 'Powis Castle' wormwood is covered with soft hairs.

Artemisia 'Powis Castle'
'POWIS CASTLE' WORMWOOD

NATIVE HABITAT Garden hybrid

HARDINESS ZONES 6 (5 with protection) to 8

'Powis Castle' wormwood is a stout shrub grown as a perennial that quickly reaches 3 to 4 feet tall and wide. The deeply lobed, aromatic silver foliage is covered with soft hairs, making it a lovely, luminescent addition to the garden. Plants flower in late summer on wood over a year old, which means they will not flower if pruned regularly every year. This is no hardship, as the plant's main attribute is its foliage.

HOW TO GROW Plant wormwood in well-drained average sandy or loamy soil. Avoid overly rich soils, which encourage weak growth. Keep the plants well shaped with occasional pruning throughout the growing season. With age, the old stems become quite woody, and the clump may fall open at the center. Cut plants back by at least half in late winter or early spring; very woody clumps may be cut back to the ground if they are losing vigor. In the north, this plant dies back to the ground annually.

RELATED SPECIES *Artemisia ludoviciana,* prairie sage, is a spreading perennial with soft, milky-silver leaves on 2- to 4-foot stems. Plants may be over-enthusiastic in rich soils. Zones 3 to 8.

COMPANION PLANTS Use wormwood to add structure and mass to large borders of pastel colors. Ornamental onions (*Allium*), coneflowers (*Echinacea*), catmints (*Nepeta*), and yarrows (*Achillea*) are good companions. A contrasting purple-foliaged smoke bush (*Cotinus coggygria* 'Velvet

Like other milkweeds, butterfly weed will bring lots of butterflies to your garden.

Cloak') makes an exciting display in the company of bearded irises, magenta *Geranium* 'Ann Folkard', and *Allium* 'Purple Sensation', followed by burgundy daylilies like *Hemerocallis* 'Minstrel Boy', purple coneflower (*Echinacea purpurea*), and maroon-flowered *Knautia macedonica*.

Asclepias tuberosa
BUTTERFLY WEED

NATIVE HABITAT Meadows, prairies, and roadsides throughout eastern and central North America

HARDINESS ZONES 3 to 9

Butterfly weed is a mecca for butterflies, especially monarchs, whose caterpillars feed exclusively on milkweed leaves. A single clump sets a garden aflutter with wings over fiery orange flowers. This tough summer bloomer produces a profusion of unusual waxy flowers with five reflexed (curving backward) petals borne in flat-topped terminal clusters. Inflated, candlelike seed pods split to release seeds that are carried away by the breeze on silken parachutes.

HOW TO GROW Butterfly weed grows along roadsides and in other tough spots, so give it average loamy or sandy soil. Plants tolerate both acidic and limy soils and seem to perform equally well in sand and heavy clay as long as it is well drained. Mature clumps grow 2 to 3 feet tall and wide from a thick taproot that resents disturbance once established. Like other milkweeds, it is easily grown from fresh seed sown outdoors.

RELATED SPECIES *A. exaltata*, poke milkweed, is a handsome plant that grows to 4 feet tall with oval leaves and rounded axillary clusters of bicolor green and rose flowers. Zones 4 to 7.

COMPANION PLANTS Butterfly weed is equally at home in informal or formal landscapes. Place plants at the front or middle of the border in combination with yarrows (*Achillea*), blanket flowers (*Gaillardia*), sundrops (*Oenothera*), and gold-variegated yucca. Add sage (*Salvia* 'East Friesland') and catmints (*Nepeta*) for a bright color contrast. Plant a broad sweep or scattered clumps in a meadow or restored prairie with native grasses and wildflowers.

Calamintha nepeta (nepetoides)
SAVORY CALAMINT

NATIVE HABITAT Meadows, roadsides, and scrub throughout Europe to Russia and North Africa

HARDINESS ZONES 3 to 9

Calamint is a breath of fresh air during the dog days of summer. This dainty, long-blooming perennial forms

tight, rounded mounds to 1½ feet tall and wide that bloom from early summer through hard frost. The upright sprays of small flowers appear white in high summer but take on a lavender cast in the cooler days of autumn. The small, rounded leaves are pungent with the scent of pennyroyal when crushed.

HOW TO GROW Light, rich, well-drained close-to-neutral soil suits it best, but calamint is a cinch to grow in almost any soil that is not soggy. Give it a spot in full sun or partial shade. Plants thrive on neglect and demand nothing from the gardener, providing continuous, pest-free bloom in return. If blooming slows in late summer, cut plants back by half to encourage fresh growth and renewed flowering.

RELATED SPECIES *Calamintha grandiflora,* large-flowered calamint, is stouter in foliage and flower. Rounded, toothed hairy leaves clothe 3-foot stems along with ½-inch white flowers.

COMPANION PLANTS Calamint combines beautifully with most perennials and shrubs, but it was made for pastel color schemes. Pair it with larger flowers like winecups (*Callirhoe*), balloon flowers (*Platycodon*), coneflowers (*Echinacea*), and daylilies (*Hemerocallis*) for contrast in form and texture. Add a few wands of blazing stars (*Liatris*) or veronicas for height and excitement. Use in a mass planting with alliums and other summer bulbs or as a skirt weaving among shrubs like beauty berry (*Callicarpa americana*) and smoke bush (*Cotinus coggygria*).

Calamint blooms from early summer through hard frost.

Winecups spread to form a flowering mat that's several feet wide. To promote fresh growth, cut stems back as flowering slows.

Callirhoe involucrata

WINECUPS, PURPLE POPPY MALLOW

NATIVE HABITAT Prairies, roadsides, and savannas from North Dakota and Montana south to Missouri and New Mexico

HARDINESS ZONES 4 to 9

Winecups carpet the ground with sumptuous chalices of rosy burgundy. This sprawling to creeping plant spreads to form a mat from 2 to 4 feet wide. The attractive, handlike leaves are deeply dissected into 5 to 7 toothed lobes. The richly colored cupped flowers are carried singly above the foliage. Plants begin blooming in mid- to late spring and flower profusely for several months on new growth. *Callirhoe involucrata* is considered invasive in some areas. See "Invasive Plants," on page 35, to determine which plants could be problematic in your area.

HOW TO GROW Plant in average, well-drained loamy or sandy soil in full sun or light shade. Set out young plants in their final position, as they do not move well due to their branched taproots. In rich soils, plants form dense clumps that may need thinning to keep them from swamping other plants. Cut stems back as flowering slows to promote fresh growth.

RELATED SPECIES *Callirhoe digitata*, standing winecups, is an upright to sprawling plant standing 1 to 4 feet tall with wiry stems sparsely clothed in deeply dissected, spidery foliage. The 1- to 2-inch flowers are carried singly or in few-flowered clusters. Zones 4 to 9. *C. triangulata,* poppy mallow, is similar in habit to winecups, but the undivided leaves are broadly triangular to heart-shaped with rounded lobes. Deep purple-red flowers are carried in open clusters in the leaf axils at the ends of 1- to 2-foot stems. Zones 4 to 8.

COMPANION PLANTS Winecups are consummate weavers, best used to knit plantings together at the front of a bed. The trailing stems creep between or over clumps of plants, and flowers pop up here and there. In formal garden situations, combine them with bold foliage plants like yuccas, bear's breeches (*Acanthus*), lamb's ears (*Stachys lanata*), and bearded irises. In meadow or prairie gardens, plant them with milkweeds (*Asclepias*), sundrops (*Oenothera*), asters, and grasses. For a long-flowering carpet, let them drape elegantly over a rock wall.

Centranthus ruber
JUPITER'S BEARD, RED VALERIAN
NATIVE HABITAT Meadows, rock outcroppings, and beaches around the Mediterranean

HARDINESS ZONES 5 (4 with protection) to 8

Jupiter's beard delights all who see it growing from a paper-thin crack in a garden wall. This plant is the essence of early summer in English gardens, inspiring American visitors to try to replicate the magic at home. Domed terminal (at the tip of the stem) and axillary (at the junction between stem and leaf) clusters of small pink, rose, coral-red, or white flowers are carried on the upper half of erect branching stems. The smooth leaves are blue-green and quite attractive during and after flowering. Plants grow $1\frac{1}{2}$ to 3 feet tall and 2 feet wide. This plant is considered an invasive exotic on the West Coast. Gardeners who live in areas where Jupiter's beard has proven invasive should refrain from growing it. For more information, see "Invasive Plants," on page 35.

HOW TO GROW Red valerian is easily grown on average loamy to sandy neutral or limy soils. Plants also tolerate saline soils and sea spray, and they thrive in rock gardens and stone walls, seemingly in no soil at all. They will grow in moist, well-drained soils in cooler regions but shrink from excessive summer heat and humidity. Shear plants after flowering if they become floppy. Plants may self-sow freely under favorable conditions.

RELATED SPECIES *Centranthus ruber* var. *coccineus* ('Coccineus') has deep scarlet flowers. *C.* var. *roseus* 'Roseus' has rose-red flowers. Zones 5 to 8.

COMPANION PLANTS The cerise flowers can be difficult to combine with other colors but are perfect with neutral rock surfaces. Strong blues, purples, and yellows hold their own against the red, as do white flowers. In the border plant them with yarrows (*Achillea*), irises, asters, spiky catmints (*Nepeta*), veronicas, and salvias, as well as sundrops (*Oenothera*) and coreopsis.

Dianthus gratianopolitanus
CHEDDAR PINKS
NATIVE HABITAT Cliffs and rock outcroppings throughout Europe

HARDINESS ZONES 3 to 9

Cheddar pinks spread quickly, forming floriferous clumps with a spicy scent.

Pinks are the darlings of the early-summer garden. Their spicy scent and ragged petals are beloved for their old-fashioned charm. This low, carpeting perennial grows 9 to 12 inches tall, forming bushy rosettes of silvery lance-shaped leaves. Carried singly or in pairs, the showy rose-pink spring flowers are produced in such profusion that they cover the foliage. This is a popular species with many choice cultivars.

HOW TO GROW Plant cheddar pinks in moist to dry, well-drained alkaline to slightly acidic soil. They spread quickly to form floriferous clumps but may be short-lived, so divide the clumps every two to three years to keep them vigorous. Judicious deadheading will keep plants in bloom for six weeks or more. Good air circulation and sharp drainage are the best precautions against rot and disease problems.

RELATED SPECIES *Dianthus deltoides,* maiden pinks, is a mat-forming plant with a profusion of small, single pink or rose flowers borne one to a stem. Zones 3 to 9. *D. plumarius,* cottage pinks, is a cushion-forming plant with grasslike basal leaves and two to five fragrant white or pink flowers per stem. Zones 3 to 9. *D. superbus,* lilac pinks, forms open mounds of grasslike leaves topped with fragrant, deeply cut, ragged flowers in lilac, pink, or white. Zones 4 to 8.

COMPANION PLANTS Pinks call to mind the eclectic cottage gardens of another generation. Place them along the edge of beds and borders where their mat-forming foliage makes a neat, attractive groundcover. Contrast their fine texture with gray-leafed *Artemisia* 'Valerie Finnis' or the broad leaves of lamb's ears (*Stachys lanata*). Let small-leafed thymes weave among the cushionlike clumps. Add height with beard tongues (*Penstemon*), sedums, culinary sages, and ornamental grasses like fescue (*Festuca*) and moor grass (*Molinia*). *Caryopteris* × *clandonensis* is a good shrubby companion.

Echinops ritro
GLOBE THISTLE

NATIVE HABITAT Rocky slopes and scrub from the Mediterranean to Siberia

HARDINESS ZONES 3 to 8

Globe thistle is an architectural gem in both foliage and flower. The plant offers drama as a specimen or in a mass planting. A coarse, erect perennial, it has lobed, spiny leaves and spherical heads of tightly packed

An architectural gem, globe thistles are long-lived, given excellent drainage.

steel-blue midsummer flowers in open terminal clusters. From a thick, branching taproot the long-lived plants grow to 3 feet wide, producing several stout stems that are between 2 and 4 feet tall.

HOW TO GROW Plant globe thistles in average to rich sandy or loamy soil. Once established, the plants are tolerant of diverse soils and moisture levels. Good drainage is essential, especially in winter. Globe thistles are quite drought-tolerant, but heavy, wet soils are sure death. They rarely need dividing, but you can either lift the huge roots carefully in autumn or remove an auxiliary rosette from the plant without disturbing the entire clump.

RELATED SPECIES *Echinops exaltatus* is a massive plant for large gardens, with superb form and large greenish-white flower heads on 6-foot plants. Zones 4 to 8.

COMPANION PLANTS Globe thistles add flair to any planting. Position them

near the middle or back of the border in combination with other dramatic, drought-tolerant perennials such as yarrows (*Achillea*), silphiums, elecampanes (*Inula*), and Jerusalem sage (*Phlomis*). Contrast the bold form with fine-textured plants, such as Russian sage (*Perovskia atriplicifolia*), calamints, autumn sage (*Salvia greggii*), silky gray willow (*Salix repens* var. *argentea*), and ornamental grasses.

Eryngium bourgatii
MEDITERRANEAN SEA HOLLY
NATIVE HABITAT Spanish Pyrenees

HARDINESS ZONES 5 to 8

Sea holly adds a dramatic touch with its architectural foliage and spherical blue flower heads surrounded by stiff, spiny silver-blue bracts. The elaborately incised bracts are what command attention from this summer-blooming species. Plants grow 1 to 2 feet tall on stout, compact stems clothed in pinnately divided (like a feather) leaves with prominent white veins.

HOW TO GROW Plant sea hollies in average sandy to loamy, well-drained soil. They tolerate all manner of adversity, thriving in gravel and pure sand in the full summer sun. Plants seldom need division. Seedlings often appear spontaneously around the garden and should be moved while they are young, as the fleshy taproot resents disturbance.

RELATED SPECIES *Eryngium amethystinum,* amethyst sea holly, the hardiest of the blue-flowered species, has small steel-blue heads surrounded by sparse, narrow blue bracts. The stems are also blue. The basal leaves are pinnately divided. Zones 2 to 8. *E. giganteum,* giant sea holly, is a coarse plant with green flower heads and broad, spiny, gray-blue bracts. The basal leaves are heart-shaped. This species is a biennial or short-lived perennial. Zones 4 to 8. *E. yuccifolium,* rattlesnake master, is a

striking native wildflower with leafy rosettes of lance-shaped, gray-green leaves and tall stout stalks crowned by open clusters of pale green heads with inconspicuous bracts. Plants prefer rich, moist soil. Zones 4 to 9. *E. × zabelii,* Zabel's sea holly, is a showy plant with bright blue flower heads and bracts mounded atop branching stems. Zones 4 to 8.

COMPANION PLANTS Sea hollies are architectural gems that add zest to any garden. Combine them with soft floriferous perennials for contrast such as calamints, sea lavender (*Limonium latifolium*), flowering spurge (*Euphorbia corollata*), or Russian sage (*Perovskia atriplicifolia*). Contrast the rounded form with erect spikes of Culver's root (*Veronicastrum virginicum*) and blazing stars (*Liatris*).

Euphorbia characias
MEDITERRANEAN SPURGE

NATIVE HABITAT Open woods and rocky slopes around the Mediterranean

HARDINESS ZONES 7 to 9

The huge acid-yellow trusses of Mediterranean spurge glow in the evening light and shine dramatically in the spring sun. This succulent perennial is a valuable addition to the garden for its attractive blue-green foliage and colorful bracts surrounding inconspicuous black-eyed yellow flowers. The stout leafy clumps, 3 to 4 feet tall and wide, have thick stems with caustic milky sap that flows freely when the stems are damaged.

HOW TO GROW Plant Mediterranean spurge in well-drained, average to

Mediterranean sea holly grows from a fleshy taproot and resents disturbance once established.

rich soil in full sun or partial shade. This easy-care perennial is quite drought-tolerant once established, but it may be short-lived. As it self-sows freely, there are always young plants to replace older ones.

RELATED SPECIES *Euphorbia characias* subsp. *wulfenii,* thought by some to be a separate species, is similar but has larger, eyeless yellow flowers. Zones 7 to 9. *E. corollata,* flowering spurge, forms open clumps to 2 feet tall resembling flat-topped baby's breath (*Gypsophila*) but with creeping stems. The foliage of this American native turns red to pink in autumn. Zones 3 to 8. *E. polychroma,* cushion spurge, is a popular species forming compact mounds of bright yellow flowers in early spring. The clumps remain attractive throughout the growing season and turn red and orange in autumn. Zones 4 to 8.

COMPANION PLANTS Mediterranean spurge holds center stage when in bloom and is an attractive foliage plant throughout the year. Combine it with plants that will complement rather than upstage its dramatic presence. Choose a carpet of spring bulbs such a daffodils, grape hyacinths, glory-of-the-snow (*Chionodoxa*), and *Ipheion,* accented with silvery artemisias. Use a large drift in front of flowering shrubs or dwarf conifers.

Festuca glauca
BLUE FESCUE
NATIVE HABITAT Meadows, scrub, and open woods in southern France

HARDINESS ZONES 4 to 8

Like a blue sea urchin, this decorative grass accents rock gardens and borders alike. Dense tufts of graceful threadlike leaves form rounded mounds 6 to 10 inches tall, accented by airy plumes held above the foliage in early summer. This cool-season grass begins growth early in the year and rests during the summer after the seed ripens.

HOW TO GROW Blue fescue demands a well-drained position in full sun or light shade. Plants tolerate sandy or loamy soils on the sweet side, but they may be short-lived, especially in soggy soil. Winter moisture and summer humidity promote decline, and clumps tend to die out at the center if conditions aren't perfect. Plants look best throughout the summer and autumn if the faded flowers are removed. Shear them in late winter to promote fresh growth. In areas with high summer heat and humidity, a gravel mulch will help cool the roots and improve air circulation.

COMPANION PLANTS Blue fescue is often employed as a groundcover in mass plantings. Though it looks spectacular used this way, its short-lived nature under less than ideal conditions may compromise the integrity of the planting. Combine plants with sedums, yuccas, and other drought-tolerant plants in rock gardens and gravel beds.

Gaura lindheimeri
WHITE GAURA
NATIVE HABITAT Open woods, prairies, and roadsides in Louisiana and Texas

HARDINESS ZONES 5 to 9

Like a swarm of insects, the small white flowers of gaura seem to buzz on wiry stems above the foliage. This buoyant, shrubby perennial has erect 3- to 4-foot spires carrying 1-inch white flowers well above the deep

Choose airy white gaura to add motion to a border or informal planting. In warmer regions native gaura will bloom from spring through frost.

green linear foliage. Aging flowers fade to pale rose. In the North, plants bloom in late summer and fall, but in warmer regions they may bloom from spring through frost. Mature plants form a deep taproot.

HOW TO GROW Plant gaura in dry to moist, well-drained soil. Established plants are drought-tolerant, but they bloom longer with even moisture. Gaura is prized by gardeners in warm regions because this native perennial tolerates steamy heat and still blooms well, unlike many other drought-tolerant species. Plants seldom need division and will politely self-sow.

COMPANION PLANTS Choose gaura to add motion to containers, borders, and informal gardens, or use it as a specimen plant. The airy, dancing spikes blend with most perennials, grasses, and shrubs. Employ it as a weaver to tie together bold plants such as daylilies (*Hemerocallis*) and coneflowers (*Echinacea*). In the autumn garden combine gaura with a profusion of asters to add a spiky form to the floriferous mounds.

Helictotrichon sempervirens
BLUE OAT GRASS

NATIVE HABITAT Rocky slopes and open woods of the western Mediterranean

HARDINESS ZONES 4 to 8

This grass's dense, spiky mounds of powder-blue lances create an enchanting effect in the evening garden among pale-flowered perennials. It is prized for its decorative 1-foot evergreen leaves as well as the tall, airy plumes atop wiry 3-foot stems that

Give blue oat grass plenty of room, so individual clumps can develop to their full, nearly spherical form.

wave above the rosettes. A cool-season plant, this grass begins growth in early spring and flowers in late spring and early summer.

HOW TO GROW Plant blue oat grass in sandy to loamy, moist to dry, well-drained soil in full sun or light shade. Excessive soil moisture, especially in winter, promotes root rot, leading to fast decline. In areas with humid summers, plants may develop foliar rust, which produces orange growth on the leaves and may disfigure the plant. Good air circulation helps keep plants healthy in warmer zones. Remove the flowers as they fade, or they will collapse haphazardly and compromise the plant's beauty. Shear the clumps to smooth mounds in late winter to allow the fresh growth to emerge.

COMPANION PLANTS Blue oat grass is a dramatic plant best used as a single accent or in a small group. Give the clumps plenty of room so they can develop their full, nearly spherical form. Combine them with low, carpet-forming thymes, verbenas, winecups (*Callirhoe*), and other plants that will not hide the foliage. In the background, place catmints (*Nepeta*), alliums, asters, and colorful shrubs.

Iris Bearded Hybrids
BEARDED IRIS
NATIVE HABITAT Garden hybrids

HARDINESS ZONES 3 to 10

Gardeners have had a love affair with iris for centuries. The exotic iris flower is composed of six segments: three bearded falls ringing three erect standards. Flowers tower on thick stems above stiff flat fans of foot-tall gray-green leaves. Plants grow from thick creeping rhizomes.

Based on their mature size and the species that were used to create the hybrids, bearded iris are divided into three groups: Group 1: Tall Bearded; Group 2: Intermediate Bearded; and Group 3: Dwarf Bearded.

HOW TO GROW Thick, water-storing rhizomes make irises extremely drought-tolerant. Give bearded irises evenly moist but well-drained, humus-rich limy or slightly acidic soil in full sun or light shade. In soggy soils irises may succumb to rhizome rot or bacterial soft rot. The plants are susceptible to attacks by the iris borer, which travels down the leaves and hollows out the rhizome. Dig up infected plants and destroy the fat pink grubs by hand.

COMPANION PLANTS Bearded irises are prized for borders, where their frilly, colorful flowers combine well with early-summer perennials and shrubs. Plant them on a dry bank

where you can enjoy the flowers and forget about them for the rest of the year.

Lavandula angustifolia
COMMON LAVENDER

NATIVE HABITAT Rocky slopes and open woods around the Mediterranean and Spanish Pyrenees

HARDINESS ZONES 5 to 9

Fragrant in foliage and flower, lavender is a popular small shrub grown as a perennial for its garden beauty and its use both cut and dried. Dense clumps 2 to 3 feet tall and wide sport aromatic, evergreen soft gray-green needlelike leaves. In high summer, erect spikes of lavender-blue flowers are held in profusion above the foliage. On warm summer days, the smell of lavender oil permeates the garden.

HOW TO GROW Plant common lavender in well-drained average to rich, close-to-neutral soil. Good drainage and sweet soil are essential for long-term survival, especially where winters are cold and wet. Established plants can endure extremely dry conditions. Prune off any shoots damaged by winter cold and reshape the plants in spring. Give old plants a hard shearing every few years to encourage fresh growth and renewed flowering. Propagate lavender from tip cuttings taken off new growth in fall.

COMPANION PLANTS Use lavender as a hedge, to edge beds, and to create patterned parterres and intricate knot gardens. In garden beds combine them with pinks (*Dianthus*), salvias, beard tongues (*Penstemon*), yarrows

Thick, water-storing rhizomes make bearded irises extremely drought-tolerant. Left: *Iris* **'Stepping Out'.**

(*Achillea*), globe thistles (*Echinops*), and sedums. Plants can be trimmed into topiaries or trained as standards in pots placed to frame an entrance or as a focal point.

Nepeta × *faassenii*
BLUE CATMINT

NATIVE HABITAT Garden hybrid

HARDINESS ZONES 4 to 8

Clouds of soft blue flowers make catmint the glory of the early-summer garden. Their profuse bloom, easy culture, and pest resistance have endeared them to low-maintenance gardeners everywhere. The soft gray-green leaves of blue catmint clothe $1^1/_2$- to 2-foot wiry stems crowned with showy tiered clusters of violet-blue flowers. The plants grow from a woody base with fibrous roots.

HOW TO GROW Plant catmint in average sandy or loamy, well-drained soil in full sun or light shade. Plants bloom

for four to six weeks in late spring and early summer. Shear clumps back by half when flowering slows, and they will quickly produce attractive new foliage and another round of flowers. In hot, humid regions, plants may rest until the cooler days of autumn before reblooming.

RELATED SPECIES *N. sibirica* 'Souvenir d'Andre Chaudron', Siberian catmint, is more erect and larger in all respects, with stems 2 to $3^1/_2$ feet tall and full spikes of showy, deep blue flowers. Zones 3 to 8. *N.* × 'Walkers Low' is a dense, wide-spreading hybrid that produces soft blue flowers all season. Zones 4 to 8.

COMPANION PLANTS Catmints are colorful plants for massing with shrubs, lining walkways and fences, edging beds, or dotting through borders. Mingle them with perennials that prefer lean soil such as winecups (*Callirhoe*), sundrops (*Oenothera*), salvias, yarrows (*Achillea*), verbena, and yuccas.

Oenothera macrocarpa
OZARK SUNDROPS, MISSOURI EVENING PRIMROSE

NATIVE HABITAT Open woods, glades, and prairies in limy soil from Illinois and Colorado, south to Missouri and Texas

HARDINESS ZONES 4 to 8

Ozark sundrops brighten up the summer garden with lemon-yellow saucers that open in the evening and fade the following afternoon. The exceptionally large, 3- to 4-inch flowers decorate sprawling to weakly upright stems 6 to 12 inches tall clothed with narrow

Profuse bloom, easy culture, and pest resistance have endeared blue catmint to low-maintenance gardeners.

Ozark sundrops open just in time for evening viewing. Individual flowers fade the following afternoon.

lance-shaped pale green leaves. Plants grow from a branched taproot.

HOW TO GROW Plant in dry to moist sandy or loamy, well-drained soil in full sun or light shade. Established plants are tough and drought-tolerant.

RELATED SPECIES *Oenothera caespitosa,* tufted evening primrose, has white rather than yellow flowers borne sparsely on low, mounded stems to 8 inches tall. The 2- to 3-inch flowers open white and fade to pink by the afternoon. Zones 4 to 7. *O. fruticosa,* sundrops, are day-flowering plants with cheery, intense yellow 1½-inch fragrant flowers in mid- to late summer. The leafy, upright to sprawling 2-foot stems bear soft, hairy 1- to 3-inch lance-shaped leaves. *O. fruticosa* subsp. *glauca* is similar, with a number of named selections. Zones 4 to 8.

O. speciosa, showy evening primrose, produces a profusion of soft pink flowers from spring to midsummer on sprawling, wiry stems to 1 foot tall. Plants spread by creeping roots and may try to take over the garden. Zones 5 to 8.

COMPANION PLANTS The rising-full-moon flowers of Ozark sundrops open just in time for evening viewing. They fit well into both formal arrangements and wild plantings combined with penstemons, cranesbills (*Geranium*), catmints (*Nepeta*), blazing stars (*Liatris*), salvias, yuccas, and grasses.

Penstemon hirsutus
HAIRY BEARD TONGUE
NATIVE HABITAT Open woods and meadows from Maine and Wisconsin south to Virginia and Kentucky

51

A foolproof species in the notoriously finicky genus *Penstemon,* hairy beard tongue, center, is equally at home in a perennial border or a rock garden.

HARDINESS ZONES 4 to 8

Hairy beard tongue is a foolproof species in a genus that is notoriously finicky. Many *Penstemon* species are cultivated, but few succeed in eastern gardens, largely because they parboil in the heat and rot in the humidity. Choose species carefully based on where you garden. Slender, erect spikes grow 1 to 2½ feet tall, bearing tiers of inflated, irregularly shaped pale violet flowers.

HOW TO GROW Plant in sandy or loamy humus-rich, well-drained soil in full sun or light shade. Good drainage, especially in winter, is essential to keep plants healthy. They slowly form dense clumps that need dividing every four to six years to stay vigorous. Plants often self-sow with abandon.

RELATED SPECIES *Penstemon barbatus,* common beard tongue, is a sturdy, adaptable species with lance-shaped gray-green foliage and stout spikes of pink to carmine flowers from 1 to 3 feet tall. Zones 4 to 8. *P. digitalis,* foxglove penstemon, is a tall species that thrives in moist soil, with shiny green leaves and erect spires of inflated white flowers. Zones 4 to 8. *P. hartwegii × P. cobaea,* gloxinia penstemon, is a lovely hybrid with huge flared red to purple flowers on erect 1½- to 2-foot stalks. Plants thrive only where summer humidity is low. Zones 5 to 7. Many hybrids of mixed parentage are also available. Some of the showiest thrive only in western states where humidity is low and winters are mild.

COMPANION PLANTS Hairy beard tongue is equally at home in a perennial border or rock garden. Combine the spiky flowers with moss phlox (*Phlox subulata*), hardy geraniums, yarrows (*Achillea*), sundrops (*Oenothera*), yuccas, and ornamental grasses.

Perovskia atriplicifolia
RUSSIAN SAGE

NATIVE HABITAT Steppes and open hillsides in eastern Europe and Turkey

HARDINESS ZONES 4 to 9

Russian sage, a broad, multibranched subshrub growing 3 to 5 feet tall and wide has gained a lot of popularity for its adaptability and long-lasting flowers. Gray buds appear atop the stems in early summer, and the blue flowers open for weeks in mid- to late summer, mingling with the small, gray-green, deeply lobed leaves. The dried stems add a touch of silver-gray to the winter border.

HOW TO GROW Plant Russian sage in well-drained sandy or loamy soil. Good drainage is essential for winter survival. In spring cut the plants back to 6 inches tall. The lower, woody stems will produce new growth. In the North, plants often die back to the soil line but resprout from the rootstock. Give plants ample room to reach their mature size.

COMPANION PLANTS Use Russian sage as an accent in a border or in mass plantings with grasses and shrubs. Place Russian sage at the middle or back of the border with intermediate-size or tall perennials. The soft blue flowers complement pink and yellow, as well as deeper blues and purples, in pastel color schemes, though they also work well with red or orange for contrast.

Salvia greggii
AUTUMN SAGE

NATIVE HABITAT Prairies, open woods, and rocky slopes of Texas and Arizona into Mexico

HARDINESS ZONES 7 to 10

Autumn sage and its hybrids are reviving interest in late-season gardening. Colorful, nonstop-blooming flowers beloved by hummingbirds make it indispensable for dry-soil gardens. A delicate shrub grown as a perennial, autumn sage grows to 3 feet tall and wide. The 1-inch, deep red flowers are carried in multiple spikes from late spring through autumn.

HOW TO GROW Plant autumn sage in well-drained sandy or loamy soils in full sun or light shade. They get leggy and flop in too much shade,

In winter the dried stems of Russian sage add a touch of silver-gray to the garden.

With its nonstop blooms beloved by hummingbirds, autumn sage is an excellent choice for a dry-soil garden.

and overly rich or moist soils also encourage flopping. Established plants are tough and extremely drought- and heat-tolerant. To revitalize old clumps, cut stems back by half (or to the ground if badly misshapen) in fall or early spring. Plants quickly resprout and resume flowering in a few months.

RELATED SPECIES *Salvia azurea,* azure sage, is a shrub-size, 3- to 4-foot-tall species with sky-blue flowers in the late-summer and autumn garden. Zones 4 to 9.

COMPANION PLANTS Autumn sage is outstanding for both garden and pot culture. In borders or prairie gardens combine autumn sage with verbenas, winecups (*Callirhoe*), lavenders, sundrops (*Oenothera*), ornamental alliums, asters, yuccas, and grasses. In a container, contrast them with filamentous bronze sedge (*Carex comans* 'Bronze'), ever-blooming *Diascia,* and bold African daisy hybrids (*Gazania*).

Schizachyrium scoparium (Andropogon scoparius)
LITTLE BLUESTEM

NATIVE HABITAT Prairies, dunes, and roadsides throughout eastern and central North America

HARDINESS ZONES 3 to 8

Little bluestem turns acres of prairie glowing bronze and glistening silver in autumn. This adaptable warm-season native grass adds fine texture and perpetual motion to meadow gardens and perennial beds alike with its lithe 1- to 3-foot stems. Plants begin growth

Trim back North American native little bluestem to just above the ground in spring to make way for new growth.

in summer, and the silvery seeds are prominently displayed late in the season on burgundy or golden stalks.

HOW TO GROW Plant little bluestem in well-drained sandy or loamy soil in full sun or light shade. Established plants have deep, water-seeking roots that hold the soil and bestow superior drought resistance. Plugs are inexpensive and establish quickly if planted before mid-autumn. Trim plants back to just above the ground in spring to make way for the new growth.

RELATED SPECIES *Andropogon ternarius,* split-beard broomsedge, is a handsome grass with tufted silvery plumes lining 1- to 2-foot bronze stems in autumn. Zones 6 to 8. *A. glomeratus,* bushy beard grass, is a showy species for moist soil with flowers aggregated

in clublike heads at the top of 2- to 4-foot stems. Zones 5 to 9.

COMPANION PLANTS In the garden, a drift of little bluestem among perennials, such as butterfly weed (*Asclepias tuberosa*), Russian sage (*Perovskia atriplicifolia*), and white gaura, is a dramatic sight. Use it as the matrix in meadow and prairie plantings where its low stature easily conforms with most community weed ordinances.

Verbascum olympicum
OLYMPIC MULLEIN

NATIVE HABITAT Open hillsides, cliffs, and scrub in Turkey

HARDINESS ZONES 6 to 8

Drama is the hallmark of the olympic mullein, whose towering candelabra

55

wands stand like sentinels keeping watch over the garden. Second-year stems of this long-lived perennial reach 3 to 5 feet from huge rosettes of oval to rounded silver-gray leaves. The branched spikes bear yellow mothlike flowers for several weeks in summer and will often rebloom in autumn if the spent stems are removed. Plants grow from stout rootstocks.

HOW TO GROW Plant olympic mullein in average well-drained sandy or loamy soil. Good drainage encourages longevity. The dried stalks are quite decorative, but unless they are removed, plants will seldom rebloom in the same season. They rarely require dividing, and self-sown seedlings will appear.

Some species of *Verbascum* are invasive. *V. thapsus,* common mullein, is considered invasive in many areas of North America. See "Invasive Plants," on page 35, to determine which plants could be problematic in your area.

RELATED SPECIES *Verbascum chaixii,* nettle-leafed mullein, is 1 to 3 feet tall, with wedge-shaped gray-green leaves and branched, spiky clusters of purple-eyed yellow flowers. Plants bloom for more than a month in early summer. *V. chaixii* var. *album* has white flowers with purple centers. Zones 4 to 8.

The tall stems of olympic mullein add height and drama to the garden.

COMPANION PLANTS With their tall, gawky stems, mulleins add a touch of the absurd to the garden. Once you develop a taste for their unique beauty, you will plant them everywhere. Combine them with other tall perennials such as catmint (*Nepeta* 'Six Hills Giant'), yarrows (*Achillea*), globe thistles (*Echinops*), meadow rues (*Thalictrum*), Russian sage (*Perovskia atriplicifolia*), wormwoods (*Artemisia*), and ornamental grasses.

COMPANION SHRUBS FOR DRY AREAS

PLANT	ZONES	BLOOM TIME	COLOR
Aesculus parviflora Bottlebrush buckeye	4 to 8	Summer	White
Amelanchier laevis Smooth serviceberry	3 to 8	Spring	White
Ceanothus 'Gloire de Versailles' Ceanothus	4 to 9	Spring/summer	Blue
Cercis canadensis Redbud	4 to 9	Spring	Pink
Chaenomeles Flowering quince	5 to 8	Winter	White, pink
Chionanthus virginicus Fringe tree	4 to 9	Spring	White
Cistus laurifolius Rock rose	7 to 10	Spring/summer	White, pink
Cornus mas Cornelian cherry	5 to 9	Winter/spring	Yellow
Enkianthus campanulatus Red-vein enkianthus	5 to 8	Spring	Red
Erica carnea Winter heath	5 to 7	Winter/spring	White, pink
Euonymus americanus Hearts-a-bustin'	5 to 9	Summer	Green
Exochorda racemosa Pearl bush	4 to 8	Spring	White
Fothergilla major Witch alder	5 to 9	Spring	White
Franklinia alatamaha Franklin's tree	5 to 8	Late summer	White
Halesia diptera Silverbell	4 to 8	Spring	White
Hamamelis vernalis Ozark witch-hazel	4 to 9	Winter	Yellow
Hydrangea quercifolia Oak-leaf hydrangea	5 to 9	Summer	White
Ilex opaca American holly	5 to 9	Summer	White
Jasminum humile Italian yellow jasmine	7 to 9	Summer	Yellow
Kerria japonica Japanese kerria	4 to 9	Spring	Yellow
Lespedeza thunbergii Thunberg bushclover	4 to 9	Autumn	White, purple
Philadelphus coronarius Mock orange	3 to 8	Spring/summer	White
Rhododendron austrinum Florida azalea	6 to 9	Spring	Yellow, orange
Rhododendron periclymenoides Pinxter bloom	5 to 8	Spring	Pink
Rhus copallina Winged sumac	4 to 9	Summer	White
Rosmarinus officinalis Rosemary	7 to 10	Spring/summer	Lavender
Vaccinium corymbosum Highbush blueberry	3 to 8	Spring	White
Viburnum acerifolium Maple-leaf viburnum	4 to 8	Spring	White
Viburnum carlesii Koreanspice viburnum	4 to 8	Spring	Pink
Viburnum rafinesquianum Southern arrowwood	4 to 9	Early summer	White
Vitex agnus-castus Chaste tree	5 to 9	Summer	Blue, white

Perennials for Moist Areas

Agastache 'Tutti-frutti'
'TUTTI FRUTTI' ANISE HYSSOP

NATIVE HABITAT Garden hybrid

HARDINESS ZONES 5 (with protection) to 9

What a cutie! 'Tutti-frutti', a shocking-pink blooming machine, is one of the new darlings of the perennial trade. Unknown just a few years ago, this sensational hybrid has brilliant rose-pink flowers in tiered whorls topping 3- to 4-foot stems. Long flowering combines with drought and heat tolerance to make a nearly perfect perennial, hence its meteoric rise. As an added bonus, the flowers are edible! So, you don't like hot pink? Try one of the golden-orange or salmon-colored selections.

HOW TO GROW Rich, moist but well-drained soil in full sun or light shade is the key to success with this easy, fast-growing plant, which tolerates drought but quickly succumbs in soggy soil. 'Tutti-frutti' performs equally well in containers and flower beds.

RELATED SPECIES *Agastache rupestris,* rock anise hyssop, has fuzzy, fragrant lance-shaped leaves and wiry stems topped by whorls of salmon-orange flowers. Like others in this group, plants don't skip a beat in summer heat. *A. foeniculum,* anise hyssop, is a hardy prairie native with bold blue flower spikes and quilted, anise-scented leaves. Zones 3 to 8.

COMPANION PLANTS Have fun creating compelling color combinations with 'Tutti-frutti'. Bright, shocking color schemes fall into place with boisterous partners like magenta winecups (*Callirhoe*), black-eyed *Geranium* 'Ann Folkard', joe-pye weed (*Eupatorium purpureum*), and verbenas. Tender perennials are great companions too, especially coleus, cannas, pentas, and dahlias. Contrast the tall spikes with purple-leafed shrubs like smokebush (*Cotinus coggygria* 'Velvet Cloak') or *Physocarpus* 'Diablo'.

Allium schoenoprasum
CHIVES

NATIVE HABITAT Damp meadows, often in the mountains in North America and Europe

HARDINESS ZONES 3 to 8

This bulbous perennial looks as good as it tastes. In ornamental gardens culinary chives are grown for their profusion of spherical pink to mauve flower clusters in early summer. Chives produce fleshy, hollow edible leaves 10 to

Chives are one of the many attractive edible *Allium* species.

20 inches tall from pungent bulbs. *A. schoenoprasum* is but one of dozens of ornamental *Allium* species.

HOW TO GROW Chives thrive in average to rich, moist, well-drained soils in full sun. Alliums are available as potted stock, though many species are sold as dormant bulbs in fall. Plants bloom for a month or more. Pluck out faded flowers to keep the display neat, or cut the entire clump to the ground when all the flowers have faded.

RELATED SPECIES *Allium cernuum,* nodding onion, is aptly named for its nodding, tear-shaped buds that open into flowery pink clusters on 1- to 2-foot stalks in summer. Zones 4 to 9. *A. senescens,* German garlic, produces rounded 10- to 12-inch-tall clusters of mauve flowers borne above dull green leaves in midsummer. Zones 3 to 9. *A. tuberosum,* garlic chives, is a floriferous plant with attractive rosettes of flattened leaves and erect stems 1½ to 2 feet tall, bearing starry white flowers in late summer. Plants self-sow rampantly, so be sure to deadhead. Zones 4 to 8.

COMPANION PLANTS Chives seem to blend with everything. Their pinky-mauve color looks good with pastels as well as strong reds and purples. Plant them toward the front of the border with cranesbills (*Geranium*), catmints (*Nepeta*), coreopsis, yarrows (*Achillea*), and ornamental grasses. Try them in the cutting garden or mix them with herbs.

Alstroemeria 'Sweet Laura'
PERUVIAN LILY
NATIVE HABITAT Garden hybrid

HARDINESS ZONES 6 to 10

Peruvian lilies are beloved cut flowers, but until recently they were too

All summer long, hardy *Alstroemeria* hybrids produce perfumed flowers.

heat- and cold-sensitive to be of much use in most gardens, thriving only on the West Coast. The University of Connecticut changed all that with the introduction of a suite of hardy hybrids. Though their flowers are smaller than those of their tender relations, they are showy and long-lasting. 'Sweet Laura' is a floriferous hybrid with perfumed yellow-orange, red-spotted flowers that flair outward. Plants bloom all summer and well into autumn on 30-inch stems. Within just a few seasons they form broad 2- to 3-foot clumps.

HOW TO GROW Give 'Sweet Laura' a spot in humus-rich, evenly moist soil in full sun to light shade. Plants spread, producing new flowering stems from an ever-widening clump throughout the season. When the clumps begin to die out in the middle, dig them up, enrich the soil, and replant the healthy portions.

RELATED SPECIES *Alstroemeria psittacina,* parrot lily, performs admirably where summers are hot and winters get cold. What you gain in hardiness you give up in show, as the attractive 1-inch red and green flowers are produced stingily and barely open. Zones 7 to 10. *A. ligtu* and its hybrids are popular cut flowers, and on the West Coast they are excellent garden plants that offer showy flowers over a long summer and autumn season in various shades of yellow, orange, and pink. Zones 8 to 10.

COMPANION PLANTS Use the soft-textured leaves and colorful flowers to weave together plantings of garden phlox, daylilies (*Hemerocallis*), and other summer perennials. Bold-textured elephant ears (*Colocasia*) and colorful dahlias are perfect companions. In the autumn, the orange flowers contrast beautifully with blue and purple asters.

Amsonia tabernaemontana
WILLOW BLUESTAR

NATIVE HABITAT Open woods, roadsides, and stream banks from New Jersey to Illinois south to Georgia and Texas

HARDINESS ZONES 3 to 9

Willow bluestar is a tough plant with luxuriant willowlike foliage and clusters of starry, five-petaled steel- to sky-blue flowers that crown 3- to 3½-foot stems in spring. The bright green lance-shaped leaves remain attractive all season, turning yellow to fiery orange in the fall. The summer fruits resemble green cigars.

HOW TO GROW Plant willow bluestar in average to rich, moist soil in full sun or partial shade. Plants attain gigantic proportions when mature. Keep them a manageable size and promote compact growth by shearing them down to 6 to 8 inches high after flowering.

RELATED SPECIES *Amsonia tabernae-montana* var. *montana,* dwarf bluestar, forms compact clumps to 1½ feet tall with proportionately larger clusters of waxy flowers. This diminutive variety is especially useful in small gardens or in tight places. Zones 3 to 9. *A. hubrichtii,* Arkansas blue star, is a textural gem for the summer and autumn garden. Billowing clumps with narrow, linear foliage are topped with domed clusters of pale blue flowers. The striking peach to golden fall color is guaranteed to stop you dead in your tracks. *A. ludoviciana,* Louisiana blue star, forms stout clumps to 3 feet wide, sporting broad, dull green leaves with felted backs and large flowers. Zones 6 to 9.

To promote compact growth, shear native willow bluestar after flowering.

Spreading by creeping underground stems, Japanese anemones can be rather aggressive in the garden, but they are easily divided after flowering.

COMPANION PLANTS Willow bluestar adds texture and structure to the garden. Contrast its rounded form with spreaders like cranesbills (*Geranium*) and upright plants such as garden phlox, meadow rues (*Thalictrum*), joe-pye weed (*Eupatorium*), asters, and sunflowers (*Helianthus*). Use a mass planting as a hedge or low screen along a drive.

Anemone × hybrida
JAPANESE ANEMONE
NATIVE HABITAT Garden hybrid

HARDINESS ZONES 4 (with protection) to 9

Like porcelain chalices, the five-petaled flowers of Japanese anemones shimmer on tall stalks that sway with the slightest breeze. Most of the plants sold as Japanese anemones are cultivars of hybrid origin. They are taller than their wild parents, varying in height from 3 to 5 feet. Single and double flowers range in color from white to pink and rose.

HOW TO GROW Give these beauties rich, evenly moist soil in sun or light shade. They will tolerate damp conditions. Spreading by creeping underground stems, they can be rather aggressive. Divide clumps in spring or after flowering. In Zone 4, plants are subject to freeze damage where snow cover is inadequate, so mulch as a precaution.

RELATED SPECIES *Anemone tomentosa* 'Robustissima' is the earliest of the anemones to bloom. Cheery silvery-pink flowers with a rosy reverse open in profusion in late summer. Zones 3 to 8. *A. hupehensis,* Chinese anemone, is an excellent species with slender stalks 2 to 3 feet tall that support fragile rose-pink flowers above mostly basal leaves in late summer and fall. This species is considered invasive in Hawaii.

COMPANION PLANTS Use the stunning fall-flowering anemones en masse to enliven any late-season border. Their airy, swaying heads

61

perfectly complement the striking foliage of yuccas, New Zealand flax (*Phormium tenax*), and ornamental grasses. Good flowering companions include sunflowers (*Helianthus*), asters, goldenrods (*Solidago*), and salvias. Use them in front of flowering shrubs or at the edge of a woodland with interrupted fern (*Osmunda claytoniana*), monkshoods (*Aconitum*), and bugbane (*Actaea racemosa,* formerly *Cimicifuga racemosa*).

Aster × *frikartii*
FRIKART'S ASTER
NATIVE HABITAT Garden hybrid

HARDINESS ZONES 5 to 8

Frikart's aster is an enthusiastic bloomer with mounds of lavender-blue flowers from midsummer

through fall. This floriferous hybrid is the result of a cross between *A. amellus* and *A. thomsonii.* From slow-creeping rhizomes plants produce multiple stems 2 to 3 feet tall clothed with soft gray-green leaves.

HOW TO GROW Frikart's aster requires average to rich, evenly moist soil with excellent drainage. Excess moisture or wet soil is sure death. Plants perform best where nights are cool. They may be short-lived in cultivation.

RELATED SPECIES *Aster amellus,* Italian aster, has dense, erect stems 2 to 2½ feet tall and large, flat flowers with purple rays and a yellow center. Zones 5 to 8. *A. laevis,* smooth aster, is a pale lavender-blue aster with attractive blue-green foliage on 2- to 3½-foot stems. Zones 3 to 8. *A. novae-angliae*, New England aster, is a leafy species up to 6 feet tall with clusters of showy 2-inch purple flowers with bright yellow centers. Many selections have been made for large flower size, flower color, and compact growth. Zones 3 to 8. *A. spectabilis,* seaside aster, is a compact, leafy aster 1 to 2 feet tall with 1-inch violet flowers in summer. Zones 4 to 8.

COMPANION PLANTS Use the spreading mounds of this early aster at the front or in the middle of a border. Combine them with a variety of perennials, fall bulbs, and ornamental grasses. Contrast the blue flowers with the cerise spires of 'Firetail' knotweed (*Polygonum amplexicaule* 'Firetail'), red daylilies (*Hemerocallis*), and cherry-colored salvias, or create a classical combo with coneflowers (*Echinacea*) and black-eyed susans (*Rudbeckia*).

Frikart's aster, which begins blooming in midsummer, is one of the earliest asters to come into flower.

Baptisia australis
BLUE FALSE INDIGO

NATIVE HABITAT Open woods, meadows, and roadsides from Vermont south to North Carolina and Tennessee

HARDINESS ZONES 3 to 9

Blue false indigo is one of the stars of the early-summer garden. Erect spikes of blue, pealike flowers recall those of lupines, which do not perform well in the heat that this plant loves. Plants attain shrublike proportions, easily growing 4 feet tall and wide. The rounded clumps sport three-part, blue-green leaves that look great all summer. Dried gray seed pods persist throughout the fall and are quite showy.

HOW TO GROW Blue false indigo is a tough, long-lived plant for average to rich, moist soil in full sun or light shade. Plants grow slowly at first but eventually spread to form huge, drought-tolerant clumps. Space individual plants at least 3 feet apart and leave them in place once they are established, as they are difficult to move.

RELATED SPECIES *Baptisia alba,* white wild indigo, is a stately plant with 3- to 5-foot-tall wands of white flowers above a flattened cluster of leaves. Zones 4 to 8. *B. bracteata,* plains wild indigo or buffalo-pea, is a low, compact, spreading plant with tightly packed, drooping clusters of creamy-yellow flowers in early spring, long before the other species bloom. Zones 3 to 9. *B. perfoliata,* Georgia wild indigo, resembles a sprawling eucalyptus and is grown more for its gray-green foliage on 2-foot, vase-shaped stems than for its single yellow flowers produced at each node in early summer. Zones 7 to 9. It may be hardy in colder northern zones.

Growing slowly at first, blue false indigo eventually spreads to form a huge drought-tolerant clump.

COMPANION PLANTS Blue false indigo is a prepossessing border plant. Place it in the company of bold flowers such as peonies, oriental poppies (*Papaver orientale*), and irises for contrast. Plant airy perennials such as cranesbills (*Geranium*), winecups (*Callirhoe*), ever-blooming bleeding hearts (*Dicentra*), and 'Georgia Blue' speedwell (*Veronica peduncularis* 'Georgia Blue') around the bases of the clumps to hide the ugly "ankles" of the tall stalks.

Calamagrostis × *acutiflora*
FEATHER REED GRASS

NATIVE HABITAT Garden hybrid

HARDINESS ZONES 4 to 8

The diaphanous flowers of this graceful grass wave like curtains of pink gauze in the early-summer breeze. A cool-season grass, it greens up in early spring, forming an attractive

63

As the flowers fade, the airy inflorescences of feather reed grass tighten, becoming stiff and erect.

2-foot-high cushion above which the 3- to 4-foot-tall airy plumes open. When the flowers fade, the inflorescences tighten, becoming erect and stiff as the seeds ripen. The plumes seldom last through the fall.

HOW TO GROW Feather reed grass is easy to grow in average to rich, evenly moist soil in full sun or light shade. When the plants receive insufficient moisture, the leaves curl lengthwise. If kept too dry over a prolonged period of time, the plants will be stunted and bloom poorly. Clumps remain attractive and full for many years without division.

RELATED SPECIES *Calamagrostis brachytricha,* Korean feather reed grass, is a compact plant with tightly packed flowering stems to 4 feet held just above the foliage. The overall effect is dense and lush. Zones 4 to 8.

COMPANION PLANTS Feather reed grass is stunning intermingled with dwarf conifers or in mass plantings. Use the upright form to create unity and rhythm by repeating clumps down the full length of a border. The best companions for feather reed grass are low carpet- or mound-forming plants that will not obscure its dramatic form, such as verbena, winecups (*Callirhoe*), catmints (*Nepeta*), sundrops (*Oenothera*), and cranesbills (*Geranium*). For contrast, try alliums, Japanese anemones (*Anemone* × *hybrida*), and yuccas.

Chrysanthemum × *grandiflorum (C.* × *morifolium)*
GARDEN CHRYSANTHEMUM
NATIVE HABITAT Garden hybrid

HARDINESS ZONES 4 to 9, variable by cultivar

Hardy mums are timeless garden classics that have been in cultivation for centuries. Many hybrids have been developed, and hybridization continues today, especially for new flower forms and increased cold hardiness. Flower color runs the gamut from white through pink, rose, red, burgundy, bronze, yellow, and cream. Heads vary from daisy lookalikes, pompons, and buttons to novelty types such as spiders and spoon-petaled varieties. Flower size varies from under an inch to 6 inches across. Mums have deep green, often hairy, lobed leaves that clothe the lax 2- to 4-foot stems.

HOW TO GROW Chrysanthemums grow readily in average to rich, moist but well-drained soil. Waterlogged soil brings sure death, especially in winter. To promote compact growth, pinch individual stems or shear the clumps back by half in early summer.

To prolong flowering, regularly trim off spent flowers of thread-leaf coreopsis. In spring or fall, divide overgrown or declining plants.

But leave the plants unpruned after flowering to improve winter hardiness. Cut back leggy or dead stems in early spring to make way for new growth. Divide the clumps at least every other year to keep them healthy and attractive. Lift them in spring, discard older portions in the center, and replant into improved soil. If aphids become a problem, spray them with insecticidal soap.

RELATED SPECIES *C. zawadskii* var. *latilobum* is an extremely hardy, early-blooming mum with showy 2- to 3-inch pink flowers. The deeply lobed leaves, often edged in red, grow on 1- to 3-foot stems. Zones 4 to 9. *Tanacetum coccineum*, painted daisy, has an open form, with dissected, ferny basal leaves and 3-inch red, rose, or pale pink flowers borne singly in early summer on $1^{1}/_{2}$ - to 2-foot stems. An extract of this plant is used as an organic pesticide. Zones 3 to 7.

COMPANION PLANTS Enjoy mums in the garden with other plants or as long-lasting cut flowers. Mums are overused as carpet bedding. Instead of planting a monoculture, combine the brilliant fall flowers with asters, sedums, ornamental grasses, and shrubs.

Coreopsis verticillata
THREAD-LEAF COREOPSIS
NATIVE HABITAT Dry, open woods and roadsides from Maryland south to Arkansas and Florida

HARDINESS ZONES 3 to 9

Thread-leaf coreopsis is a showstopper. Plants form airy mounds 1 to 3 feet tall with lacy three-lobed, needle-like leaves and dozens of starry 1- to 2-inch yellow flowers borne throughout the summer.

Growing from corms, crocosmias spread enthusiastically to form leafy clumps. The fiery flowers add a splash of color to the late-summer garden.

HOW TO GROW *Coreopsis* is a tough, easy-care plant for average to rich, moist soil. To prolong flowering, regularly trim off spent flowers. Divide overgrown or declining plants in spring or fall.

RELATED SPECIES *Coreopsis auriculata,* mouse-ear coreopsis, is a low, spreading groundcover 1 to 2 feet tall with fuzzy, triangular-eared leaves and 2-inch yellow-orange flowers in spring. Zones 4 to 9. *C. lanceolata,* lance-leaf coreopsis, and the similar *C. grandiflora* are popular old-fashioned perennials with 2½-inch deep yellow flowers over 1- to 2-foot clumps of lance-shaped foliage. *C. rosea,* pink tickseed, is a low, mounded flowering machine 1 to 2 feet tall with dozens of 1-inch pink flowers with bright yellow centers. Zones 4 to 8. *C. tripteris,* tall tickseed, is a stately, stiff plant 3 to 9 feet tall with three-lobed, lance-shaped leaves

topped with wide clusters of 2-inch starry yellow flowers. Zones 3 to 8.

COMPANION PLANTS *Coreopsis* is a workhorse perennial for borders or mass plantings. Combine the bright flowers with contrasting blues and purples such as lavenders, salvias, and catmints (*Nepeta*), as well as larger plants like coneflowers (*Echinacea*) and phlox.

Crocosmia × *crocosmiiflora*
CROCOSMIA, MONTBRETIA
NATIVE HABITAT Garden hybrid

HARDINESS ZONES 5 (with protection) to 9

Crocosmias bring the colors of the sun to the summer garden. Though this hybrid was first created by French hybridizer Victor Lemoine in 1880, most modern cultivars are of English origin. The fiery-colored, flared tubular flowers are carried on 2- to 3-foot arching, zigzag stems that are good for cutting.

HOW TO GROW Plant crocosmias in moist, humus-rich soil. They grow from corms, spreading enthusiastically by runners to form leafy clumps of beautiful spear-shaped foliage. In Zones 5 and colder, lift the corms in the fall and store them indoors in a cool, dry spot. The leaves may be attacked by thrips and spider mites. Spray with insecticidal soap.

RELATED SPECIES *Crocosmia masoniorum* is a tall species with showy, fiery-orange upturned flowers on 2¹/₂- to 3-foot stems. Zones 5 to 9.

COMPANION PLANTS Crocosmias add colorful exclamation points to the late-summer garden. Dot them throughout a border among contrasting blue balloon flowers (*Platycodon*), veronicas, and salvias, or create hot-color harmonies with daylilies (*Hemerocallis*), dahlias, sneezeweed (*Helenium*), and cannas.

Digitalis grandiflora (D. ambigua)
YELLOW FOXGLOVE

NATIVE HABITAT Open woods and stream banks from Europe east to Turkey and Siberia

HARDINESS ZONES 3 to 8

Yellow foxgloves add vertical accents to summer borders with their 2- to 3-foot leafy spikes of funnel-shaped flowers. The insides of the flower tubes are streaked with brownish-purple spots. Dense, tufted basal rosettes remain green all season. All portions of the plant are poisonous.

HOW TO GROW Plant foxgloves in moist, humus-rich soil in full sun or partial shade. Though perennial, this

Unlike other species of *Digitalis*, yellow foxgloves are not considered invasive.

species loses vigor as it ages. Divide plants every few years to keep them lush. Self-sown seedlings may appear. Some foxglove species are invasive. See "Invasive Plants," on page 35, for more information on determining which plants are problematic.

COMPANION PLANTS Foxgloves mix beautifully with perennials, and they can be used in mass plantings with flowering shrubs and evergreens. Combine them with snowdrop anemones (*Anemone sylvestris*), irises, cranesbills (*Geranium*), clustered bell-flower (*Campanula glomerata*), goatsbeard (*Aruncus dioicus*), and grasses.

Echinacea purpurea
PURPLE CONEFLOWER

NATIVE HABITAT Michigan and Virginia to Georgia and Louisiana

HARDINESS ZONES 3 to 8

These purple daisies of summer are among the most popular perennials. Erect, well-branched leafy stems 2 to 4 feet tall are topped by dozens of flowers with drooping red-violet petallike rays around cone-shaped centers. Medicinally, coneflowers are used externally for alleviating skin rashes and internally for stimulating the immune system.

HOW TO GROW Purple coneflowers are tough prairie plants, thriving with little care in average to rich loamy soil in full sun or partial shade. Plants perform best with consistent moisture but are amazingly drought-tolerant once established, thanks to deep, water-storing taproots.

RELATED SPECIES *Echinacea angustifolia,* narrow-leafed coneflower, grows only 1 to 2 feet tall, with spare, lance-shaped basal leaves and nearly leafless stems topped by 2-inch heads with short, drooping rose-pink rays. Zones 3 to 8. *E. pallida,* pale purple coneflower, has stout, nearly leafless stems 3 to 4 feet tall topped by large heads of drooping pale rose rays.

Zones 4 to 8. *E. paradoxa,* yellow coneflower, is a true paradox with bright yellow flowers over tight, multi-stemmed clumps $2\frac{1}{2}$ to 3 feet tall with mostly basal leaves. Zones 4 to 8.

COMPANION PLANTS Coneflowers fit comfortably into both formal and informal gardens. They are beautiful laced through a meadow or prairie with native grasses. In borders combine them with geraniums, Shasta daisies (*Leucanthemum* × *superbum*), garden phlox, blazing stars (*Liatris*), yarrows (*Achillea*), Russian sage (*Perovskia atriplicifolia*), and grasses. The seed heads are attractive throughout the fall and winter, and birds love the seeds.

Geranium sanguineum
BLOODY CRANESBILL

NATIVE HABITAT Meadows, open woods, and dunes from Europe to Turkey

HARDINESS ZONES 3 to 8

Bloody cranesbill is a flowering carpet studded with rosy-magenta saucer-shaped flowers in early summer. Deeply incised spidery leaves clothe the sprawling 1- to 2-foot stems. The foliage turns lovely burgundy-red and orange in autumn. Hardy geraniums are called cranesbills because the seeds are held on a rigid, tapered "beak" that serves as a launching pad to project the seeds outward from the plants.

HOW TO GROW Plant bloody cranesbill in moist but well-drained humus-rich soil in full sun or partial shade. Plants are slow-spreading and form broad, deep-rooted clumps. Cut them back when flowering wanes to promote fresh growth and a new flush of bloom.

Tough North American prairie plants, purple coneflowers thrive with little care in full sun or partial shade.

When flowering wanes, cut bloody cranesbill back to promote fresh growth and a new flush of bloom. In fall the foliage turns lovely burgundy-red and orange.

RELATED SPECIES *Geranium sanguineum* var. *striatum* (*G. lancastriense*) has pale pink flowers with deep rose veins. Zones 3 to 8. *G. clarkei,* Clark's geranium, is a delicate, floriferous species with purple or white flowers on 1½-foot stems above deeply incised foliage. Zones 4 to 8. *G. psilostemon,* Armenian geranium, is a magnificent 3- to 4-foot-tall perennial with starry leaves and deep magenta flowers with black eyes. Zones 5 to 8.

COMPANION PLANTS Everything goes with geraniums. Weave them among taller plants at the front or middle of the border. Contrast their prostrate form with the spiky foliage of yuccas and Siberian irises. Plant them under flowering shrubs and small trees for dramatic effect.

Helianthus 'Lemon Queen'
LEMON QUEEN SUNFLOWER
NATIVE HABITAT Garden hybrid

HARDINESS ZONES 4 to 9

Resembling an oversize lemon parfait, this hybrid sunflower fills the late-season garden with delicious color. The stout, leafy 6- to 8-foot stems of the robust summer- and autumn-blooming plant are covered with starry, soft yellow daisylike flowers with prominent round centers. Plants grow from woody, fibrous-rooted crowns.

HOW TO GROW Sunflowers are tough, easy-to-grow plants that need ample room to spread. Plant them in moist, average to rich soil. The stout stems seldom need staking except in windy areas. Once established, they are all quite drought-tolerant.

RELATED SPECIES *Helianthus angustifolius,* swamp sunflower, always gets a wow with its 4- to 8-foot stems clothed in deep green lance-shaped leaves. In autumn the stems are crowned by elongated clusters of 3-inch bright yellow flowers with purple centers. Zones 6 to 9. *H. decapetalus,* thin-leafed sunflower, is a delicate clump-forming

69

Like all sunflowers, 'Lemon Queen' needs ample space to spread. Its stout stems seldom need staking, except in windy areas.

sunflower 4 to 5 feet tall with mounded, open clusters of 2- to 3-inch yellow flowers with yellow centers. Zones 4 to 8. *H. salicifolius,* willow leaf sunflower, is valuable for its delicate linear gray-green leaves as well as its slender upright clusters of 2-inch midautumn flowers. Plants grow 3 to 6 feet tall. Zones 4 to 8.

COMPANION PLANTS Sunflowers light up the summer and fall garden. Plant them toward the rear of the border with yuccas, garden phlox, salvias, asters, cannas, and flowering shrubs. In meadow and prairie plantings combine them with blazing stars (*Liatris*), purple coneflower (*Echinacea purpurea*), and all manner of native grasses.

Hemerocallis Hybrids
DAYLILY
NATIVE HABITAT Garden hybrid

HARDINESS ZONES 3 to 9

Daylilies are popular garden perennials that have been cultivated for food, medicine, and ornament for centuries.

The flowers are still enjoyed as a vegetable. Daylilies from Asia made their first appearance in Europe in the mid-16th century, and by the 19th century China and Japan were selling species and hybrids to customers in the United States and Europe. Today's daylilies are hybrids. Both diploids (having a single complement of chromosomes) and tetraploids (with an artificially doubled chromosome complement) are represented in plants displaying a full range of pink, red, purple, orange, and yellow selections with spidery to broad petals, blazes, extra frills, and extended bloom.

HOW TO GROW Plant tough and adaptable daylilies in average to rich, well-drained soil in full sun or light shade. They grow from thick tuberous roots that make them extremely drought-tolerant. Many tetraploids have thick, waxy flowers and need daily deadheading to keep them looking neat. Remove spent flower stalks after blooming, and cut yellowing foliage to the ground. Divide fast-

Thick tuberous roots make daylilies, which have been cultivated for centuries, extremely drought-tolerant. Above is 'King Royale'.

growing hybrids every three years or so to keep them blooming well.

RELATED SPECIES *Hemerocallis altissima,* tall daylily, is the tallest and latest-blooming species, with fragrant pale yellow flowers on 5- to 6-foot stems in summer and early fall. Zones 4 to 9. *H. dumortieri,* early daylily, opens its fragrant, funnel-shaped brown-tinged yellow flowers in late spring. Copious flowers are held just above the foliage on 1½- to 2-foot stems. Zones 2 to 9. *H. middendorffii* is a compact species with fragrant pumpkin-orange flowers held with or just above the leaves on 2½-foot stems. This species reblooms. Zones 3 to 9.

COMPANION PLANTS Daylilies are prized for their adaptability, rapid spread, and extended bloom period. Repeat bloomers such as 'Happy Returns' have infinite uses in both

The foliage color of coral bells may fade in summer and intensify in fall.

public and private landscapes. Use daylilies in mass plantings in tough spots or plant them under shrubs and trees. Clumping hybrids and species are excellent border plants combined with summer-blooming favorites.

Heuchera americana
CORAL BELLS, AMERICAN ALUMROOT

NATIVE HABITAT Open woods and rock outcroppings from New England and Michigan south to Georgia and Oklahoma

HARDINESS ZONES 4 to 9

Coral bells are like hostas for sunny gardens. Their decorative evergreen leaves are rounded to heart-shaped and may be green, yellow, or purple, mottled with gray and silver. Margins may be wavy to excessively frilly. The airy flowers are borne on narrow, upright stalks 1½ to 3 feet tall.

HOW TO GROW Plant coral bells in moist but well-drained, humus-rich soil in full sun or partial shade.

71

Foliage may bleach in hot afternoon sun. As the clumps grow, the woody rootstocks lift out of the soil and need replanting. Divide clumps every three years and replant the vigorous rosettes into amended soil. Foliage color may fade in summer and intensify in fall and winter.

RELATED SPECIES *Heuchera micrantha,* small-flowered alumroot, best known as a variable seed strain called 'Palace Purple', has deep purple-brown foliage that sets off the airy flowers to good advantage. Zones 4 to 8. *H. sanguinea,* coral bells, is the showiest species; it adds its bright crimson flowers to many selections and hybrids, including *H. × brizoides,* which, along with colorful flowers, has good foliage and heat tolerance. Zones 3 to 8.

COMPANION PLANTS Coral bells have exquisite foliage and airy flowers. Plant them as a groundcover, along a wall, or at the front of a border with low to medium-size plants such as cranesbills (*Geranium*), winecups (*Callirhoe*), pinks (*Dianthus*), catmints (*Nepeta*), yuccas, and grasses.

Kalimeris pinnatifida
MONGOLIAN OR JAPANESE ASTER

NATIVE HABITAT Open woods and meadows in Japan

HARDINESS ZONES 4 to 8

Mongolian asters have been passed around southern gardens for generations. Gardeners have always valued this understated workhorse perennial for its copious white, daisylike double flowers borne all summer and into the autumn. The 1- to 2½-foot stems are densely clothed in attractive deeply incised leaves.

HOW TO GROW Mongolian aster is easy to grow in average to rich, moist but well-drained soil in full sun or partial shade. If the profuse flower production wanes in late summer, shear plants back by half, and a new flush of flowers will carry on through autumn. If the clumps begin to lose vigor, you can easily divide them in spring.

RELATED SPECIES *Kalimeris incisa* is very similar to Mongolian aster, but the pale lavender single flowers are carried on more open 2-foot clumps. Plants bloom throughout the summer. Zones 4 to 8. *Gymnaster savatieri* is a late-season aster relative that keeps going until hard frost. It has lobed leaves and ragged pale lavender flowers on 2- to 2½-foot plants. A favorite in Europe, this plant is undeservedly scarce in North America. Clumps spread rapidly by creeping stems and

If cut back in late summer, Mongolian asters will produce a second flush of flowers that lasts through fall.

Once established, gaudy torch lilies grow with little care, forming dense clumps of evergreen, grasslike foliage.

may need to be thinned to control size. Zones 4 to 8.

COMPANION PLANTS The delicate flowers of Mongolian aster are perfect for weaving around taller or bolder plants like daylilies (*Hemerocallis*), phlox, balloon flowers (*Platycodon*), cannas, gladioli, yuccas, and salvias. Mass plantings with shrubs are also effective.

Kniphofia uvaria
TORCH LILY

NATIVE HABITAT Streamsides and open slopes in southern Africa

HARDINESS ZONES 5 to 9

Gaudy torch lilies are back in fashion at last. The flaming 3- to 5-foot wands of these showy summer perennials rise above stout tufts of long, stiff lin-

ear leaves. The color of the drooping tubular flowers varies from pure scarlet, orange, yellow, and cream to bicolors. The grasslike clumps of gray-green foliage are evergreen. Plants grow from short, creeping rhizomes with thick roots. Peak bloom is late spring and early summer, but many hybrids rebloom through autumn.

HOW TO GROW Plant torch lilies in average to rich, evenly moist but well-drained soil. Good drainage is imperative. Excess water in the soil or on the crowns will kill the plants in winter. Plants spread by short rhizomes to form dense clumps. Established plants seem indestructible and grow for years with little care.

RELATED SPECIES *Kniphofia caulescens* is a bold species that grows to 4 feet, with broad, gray-green leaves on a

73

To extend their short life spans, it's a good idea to divide shasta daisies frequently.

short trunk. The fat flower heads are orange and yellow. Zones 6 to 9.

COMPANION PLANTS Repeat the strong vertical forms of torch lilies to create rhythm in a flower bed and to lift your eyes skyward. The bold, colorful spires are like exclamation points in the late-spring and summer garden. Combine the fiery colors with yellow or orange daylilies (*Hemerocallis*), sundrops (*Oenothera*), and dahlias for harmony, or create contrast with blue catmints (*Nepeta*), balloon flowers (*Platycodon*), asters, purple salvias, and ornamental grasses.

Leucanthemum × superbum
(Chrysanthemum × superbum)
SHASTA DAISY
NATIVE HABITAT Garden hybrid

HARDINESS ZONES 3 to 8, varies by cultivar

Shastas are cheerful summer daisies, looking like roadside oxeye daisies that went to finishing school. The 2- to 3-inch pure white flowers with bright yellow centers are held on stout 1- to 3-foot leafy stalks above oblong, deep green foliage. They are popular as cut flowers and in the garden.

HOW TO GROW Plant shasta daisies in average to rich, moist but well-drained soil. Established plants are quite drought-tolerant. Deadhead to prolong flower production. Divide the plants frequently to extend their short life span. Lift the clumps in spring, discard older portions, and replant into improved soil.

RELATED SPECIES *Nipponanthemum nipponicum* (*Chrysanthemum nipponicum*), Nippon daisy, is a mounding semiwoody subshrub with 3-inch white daisies on 1- to 3-foot stalks in late summer and fall above glossy, oblong leaves. Plants tolerate seaside conditions. Zones 5 to 8. *Tanacetum parthenium*, feverfew, is an heirloom perennial with erect, bushy 2- to 3-foot stems clothed in bright green lobed foliage and topped with mounds of lacy white daisies. It blooms profusely from summer to fall. Zones 4 to 8.

COMPANION PLANTS Plant shasta daisies in the border with summer-blooming perennials such as cranesbills (*Geranium*), catmints (*Nepeta*), irises, daylilies (*Hemerocallis*), yarrows (*Achillea*), and poppies (*Papaver*), as well as grasses.

Liatris ligulistylis
MEADOW BLAZING STAR, GAYFEATHER

NATIVE HABITAT Moist black-soil prairies and the borders of marshes from Wisconsin and Alberta south to Colorado and New Mexico

HARDINESS ZONES 3 to 8

Meadow blazing star is like opium to monarch butterflies. In summer, dozens of them can be seen hanging lazily from every spike. This stout species has slender 3- to 5-foot spikes clothed in gray-green leaves that twist in a clockwise circle around the stem. The 1-inch, red-violet buttonlike heads are borne on short stalks in mid- to late summer.

HOW TO GROW Plant blazing stars in average to rich sandy or loamy, moist but well-drained soil. They may topple in the wind when grown without companion plants for support. Properly sited, they are long-lived, easy-care perennials.

RELATED SPECIES *Liatris pycnostachya,* Kansas gayfeather, is a giant species with spikes of densely packed, red-violet flower heads in summer on stiff, leafy 3- to 5-foot stems. Zones 3 to 9. *L. microcephala,* small-headed

In autumn, the foliage of purple moor grass turns golden.

blazing star, forms dense clumps of slender stems to 2 feet tall with tiny heads of red-violet flowers. Plants are drought-tolerant. *L. graminifolia* is similar but a bit more coarse. Zones 4 to 9. *L. spicata,* spike gayfeather, is one of the most popular plants in the genus. The compact 2- to 4-foot stems bear terminal spikes of deep red-violet flowers in narrow, tightly packed heads. Zones 3 to 8.

COMPANION PLANTS Blazing stars add vertical drama to formal beds as well as meadow and prairie plantings. Combine them with garden phlox, shasta daisies (*Leucanthemum* × *superbum*), balloon flowers (*Platycodon*), asters, goldenrods (*Solidago*), and ornamental grasses.

Molinia caerulea
PURPLE MOOR GRASS

NATIVE HABITAT Moist meadows and streamsides from Europe to Asia

HARDINESS ZONES 4 to 8

Purple moor grass is like a cool breeze on a sultry summer day. Airy

plumes form an open, graceful vase over tight rosettes of gray-green leaves. Plants grow to 3 feet tall with an equal spread and bloom in mid- to late summer. The foliage turns golden in autumn.

HOW TO GROW Plant in evenly moist, average to rich soil in full sun or partial shade. In hot dry areas, plants benefit from shade and require consistent moisture. This cool-season grass begins growth early in the season.

RELATED SPECIES *Molinia caerulea* ssp. *arundinacea*, tall purple moor grass, is a giant subspecies with wider leaves that form gracefully disheveled mounds. The slender inflorescences grow to 8 feet tall and together form a giant, airy vase in summer.

COMPANION PLANTS Use the airy inflorescences to add motion to borders, surrounded by low plants that will not hide the flowers. Verbenas, creeping veronica (*Veronica peduncularis* 'Georgia Blue'), winecups (*Callirhoe*), and asters are a few good choices. Use them as architectural accents or as focal points to mark an entrance or end a vista.

Paeonia lactiflora Hybrids
GARDEN PEONY
NATIVE HABITAT Garden hybrids

HARDINESS ZONES 2 to 8

Peonies are beloved flowers for summer garden color and for cutting. Their beauty, fragrance, exceptional hardiness, and easy culture have endeared them to amateurs and collectors alike. Most garden peonies are hybrids of *Paeonia officinalis* and

By planting early-, mid-, and late-season peony varieties, you will have flowers for up to six weeks.

P. lactiflora. Flower colors vary from white, cream, and yellow to pink, rose, and scarlet in singles, doubles, and pompon types.

HOW TO GROW Plant peonies in moist, humus-rich soil in full sun or light shade. Fall is the best time for planting bare-root plants, while container stock can be planted anytime. Set out the fleshy roots with the eyes (buds for next year's growth) 2 inches below the soil surface. Space rootstocks at least 3 feet apart to allow for their mature spread. Stake double-flowered selections to keep their faces out of the mud. Individual cultivars bloom for only one to two weeks, but by planting early-, mid-, and late-season varieties you will have blooms for up to six weeks.

RELATED SPECIES *Paeonia lactiflora,* Chinese peony, is a late-blooming species with single white or pink flowers on 1½- to 3-foot stalks. Zones 2 to 8. *P. mlokosewitschii,* Molly the Witch, is a compact, bushy species to 2 feet

In autumn, the tall, airy foliage of late-blooming patrinia turns burnt-orange.

tall with rounded, creamy-yellow flowers and blue-green leaves tinted with red in the spring. Zones 4 to 8. *P. officinalis,* common peony, is best known in its fully double, shell-pink form 'Rosea Superba Plena', also known as the Memorial Day peony. The wild form has single flowers. Zones 3 to 8. *P. tenuifolia,* fern leaf peony, is most often found in its deep red, double form, but the single-flowered species is also stunning. Plants grow 1 to 1½ feet tall with delicate finely divided, fan-shaped leaves. Zones 3 to 7.

COMPANION PLANTS Peonies offer both glorious flowers and excellent foliage. Plan combinations that utilize their beauty and grace throughout the season. Plant them with minor bulbs and forget-me-nots (*Myosotis*) for early spring when the ruby-red shoots are just emerging. Colorful companions include columbines (*Aquilegia*), cranesbills (*Geranium*), Siberian irises, and lady's mantle (*Alchemilla mollis*).

Patrinia scabiosifolia
PATRINIA, ELVIS EYES, LEMON LOLAPALOUSA
NATIVE HABITAT East Asia

HARDINESS ZONES 4 to 9

Patrinia forms a dreamy yellow haze in the late-season garden. This upright, airy plant produces many 3- to 6-foot stout stems clothed in large, pinnately divided (like a feather) leaves that are topped by open, branched clusters of small acid-yellow flowers in late summer and autumn. The foliage turns burnt-orange in autumn. Plants grow from a stout, branched taproot, spreading between 3 and 4 feet wide.

HOW TO GROW Plant patrinia in average to rich, moist but well-drained soil in full sun or light shade. This tough, long-lived plant thrives with little attention and seldom needs division. Self-sown seedlings may be plentiful unless the plants are deadheaded.

RELATED SPECIES *Patrinia gibbosa* has attractive divided leaves with shiny, rounded, toothed terminal leaflets. The 1- to 2-foot stems arch outward to form a vase crowned with open clusters of yellow flowers in summer. Zones 4 to 9. *P. villosa* is a low, spreading species with attractive hand-shaped basal leaves and 2- to 3-foot stalks topped in autumn with open clusters of white flowers. Zones 5 to 8.

COMPANION PLANTS Choose patrinia for the middle or back of a border for a relaxed cottage garden or as a mass planting with shrubs along a woodland edge. Combine the late-season flowers with salvias, asters, sunflowers (*Helianthus*), cannas, and grasses.

Phlomis russeliana
JERUSALEM SAGE
NATIVE HABITAT Open woods and scrub in northern Turkey

HARDINESS ZONES 5 to 8

Jerusalem sage lays out a lush carpet of broad, quilted sea-green foliage accented by 3- to 4-foot spikes of butter-yellow flowers arrayed in tiered whorls. The combined effect is dramatic in the early-summer garden. Plants creep from wiry runners to form tight tangles of foliage.

HOW TO GROW Plant Jerusalem sage in sandy or loamy, moist but well-drained soil in full sun or light shade. Plants are drought-tolerant and thrive for years with little attention. Cut the tattered leaves off in spring to make way for new growth.

RELATED SPECIES *Phlomis cashmeriana,* Kashmir sage, is a vigorous, lilac-pink-flowered species with dense tufts of basal leaves and leafy spikes to 3 feet tall. *P. samia,* Greek Jerusalem sage, is similar, with pale pink flowers. Zones 5 to 8. *P. fruticosa,* also known as Jerusalem sage, is a semiwoody shrub with erect branches 2 to 4 feet tall bearing gray-green leaves and spikes of soft yellow flowers in spring and often throughout the summer. The branches are frequently killed back in winter. Prune out dead or winter-burnt stems in early spring to make way for new growth. Zones 4 to 8. *P. tuberosa* produces erect, slender stalks to 5 feet tall bearing whorls of rosy-pink flowers over deep green basal leaves. Zones 4 to 8.

COMPANION PLANTS Combine the attractive spikes of this carefree perennial with yuccas and grasses for dramatic foliage contrast. Choose catmints (*Nepeta*), salvias, yarrows (*Achillea*), and Russian sage (*Perovskia atriplicifolia*) for flowering

To enjoy the decorative dried seed heads of Jerusalem sage in fall, be sure not to cut off spent flowers.

Garden phlox blooms for weeks on end. With careful cultivar selection, you can have phlox in bloom from June through September.

companions. The dried seed heads are decorative in autumn with the plumes of grasses.

Phlox paniculata
GARDEN OR BORDER PHLOX

NATIVE HABITAT Roadsides, low meadows, and wet woods from Pennsylvania and Illinois south to Florida and Louisiana

HARDINESS ZONES 3 to 8

Border phlox has delighted gardeners since colonial times. Large trusses of fragrant flowers in a range of purples, blues, pinks, reds, and white top 2- to 5-foot stems in summer. The flowers are tubular at the base and flair at the end to form flat five-petaled faces. Selections and hybrids are numerous, and today's hybridizers endeavor to increase mildew resistance and find new colors.

HOW TO GROW Plant garden phlox in average to rich, consistently moist soil in full sun or partial shade. Plants perform best where summers are cool. A single plant can bloom for weeks on end, so with careful cultivar selection you can have garden phlox in bloom from June through September. Plants form multistemmed dense clumps that need division every three to four years in spring. Cultivars vary in their susceptibility to mildew. (Check labels or reference books.) To avoid problems, give plants abundant moisture and good air circulation. If you discover mildew on the leaves, spray with wettable sulfur once or twice a week. Phlox are savored by rabbits and deer, which are in the habit of mowing the plants to the ground on a regular basis.

RELATED SPECIES *Phlox carolina,* thick leaf phlox, is a stout species with glossy oval leaves and elongated flower clusters from pink to purple, sometimes white. Zones 4 to 9. *P. maculata,* early phlox, is a delicate species 1 to 3 feet tall with linear foliage and narrower flower clusters. Zones 3 to 9.

COMPANION PLANTS Place border phlox along the edge of a woodland with shrubs and flowering trees, or use them in a border. Good companions include cranesbills (*Geranium*), daylilies (*Hemerocallis*), irises, bee balms (*Monarda*), shasta daisies (*Leucanthemum* × *superbum*), meadowsweet (*Filipendula*), and grasses.

Phygelius × *rectus*
CAPE FUCHSIA, CAPE FIGWORT
NATIVE HABITAT Garden hybrid

HARDINESS ZONES 7 to 10

The Pacific Northwest and the deep South have a well-kept secret, the Cape fuchsia. This exotic beauty bears dozens of nodding, slender tubular flowers with flared tips on tall, branched, 3- to 4-foot stems. Plants begin flowering in June and continue throughout the summer and autumn.

HOW TO GROW Plant Cape fuchsia in rich, evenly moist but well-drained soil. If the plants get too wet in winter they are susceptible to rot, and in extremely cold weather the rather succulent stems may be damaged. Cut stems back to live wood in spring. Plants are reliably hardy in Zone 7, but protecting the crowns in winter is a good idea. In colder zones they are terrific container plants.

RELATED SPECIES *Phygelius* × *rectus* was created by crossing pink-flowered *P. aequalis* with red-flowered *P. capensis,* two species worth growing

in their wild forms. They are similar to their hybrid offspring in form and habit, though they vary in size, with *P. capensis* reaching 4 to 6 feet, while *P. aequalis* is 2 to 3 feet at maturity. Zones 7 to 10.

COMPANION PLANTS *Phygelius* is a blooming machine in the summer and autumn border. Combine its bright, airy flower clusters with salvias, phlox, asters, goldenrods (*Solidago*), and balloon flowers (*Platycodon*), and use the stiff leaves of yuccas and ornamental grasses for contrast. Where they are not hardy, plants are perfect for containers or bedded out as annuals.

Platycodon grandiflorus
BALLOON FLOWER
NATIVE HABITAT Moist mountain meadows and streamsides throughout temperate Asia

HARDINESS ZONES 3 to 9

The huge saucer-shaped blooms of balloon flowers demand attention in the summer garden. Blue, white, or pink flowers with five starry lobes open from inflated round buds that give the plant its common name. From thick, fleshy rootstocks balloon flowers produce upright succulent stems 1 to 3 feet tall clothed in toothed, triangular leaves.

HOW TO GROW Plant balloon flowers in average to rich, evenly moist but well-drained soil in full sun or light shade. Once established, plants are tough and adaptable. New shoots emerge late in spring, so be careful not to dig into the clumps by mistake. Removing the spent flowers will promote continued bloom and keep the plants tidy. They may self-sow.

COMPANION PLANTS Combine balloon flowers with high-summer peren-

The new shoots of balloon flower emerge late in spring, so be careful not to dig into the fleshy rootstock clump by mistake.

nials such as cranesbills (*Geranium*), salvias, catmints (*Nepeta*), yarrows (*Achillea*), ornamental onions (*Allium*), bee balms (*Monarda*), and garden phlox. The dwarf varieties were developed as potted plants in Japan, and they do well in containers. Flowers last well in the vase.

Polygonum (Persicaria) amplexicaule 'Firetail'
MOUNTAIN FLEECE FLOWER, MOUNTAIN KNOTWEED

NATIVE HABITAT Moist meadows and streamsides in the Himalayas

HARDINESS ZONES 3 to 8

The mere mention of knotweed makes conservationists shudder because so many species are invasive exotics. Not mountain fleece flower, which along with a few others is a well-behaved garden plant. Erect flower spikes composed of tiny, tightly packed cerise flowers emerge from rattail buds throughout summer and autumn. Plants have jointed, or knotted, stems to 3 feet tall with puckered, lance-shaped leaves that clasp the stems.

HOW TO GROW Plant mountain fleece flower in moist, humus-rich soil in full sun or partial shade. Though plants tolerate a variety of conditions, they bloom best with consistent water and good light. Plants in full sun will flower for a month or so in early summer, then retire for the season. If the soil gets too dry the leaf margins may get crispy. Plants spread very slowly but eventually form sizeable clumps. Once established, the plants are tough and adaptable.

81

With consistent water and full sun, mountain fleece flower will bloom for a month.

RELATED SPECIES *Polygonum bistorta,* snakeweed, sports fat pink flower clusters held well above a skirt of broad paddlelike foliage. Plants demand even moisture and rich soil. Though not as rampant as its voracious brethren, snakeweed will spread to form broad clumps where it has room. Zones 3 to 8.

COMPANION PLANTS Mountain fleece flower excels in both foliage and flower in combination with astilbes, ligularias, rodgersias, ferns, and sedges in northern zones, and irises, gingers (*Hedychium*), cannas, and joe-pye weed (*Eupatorium*) farther south.

Salvia nemorosa
MEADOW SAGE

NATIVE HABITAT Meadows and rocky slopes from Europe to Central Asia

HARDINESS ZONES 3 to 8

Meadow sage brings the rich, cool hues of autumn to the early-summer garden. This shrubby member of the mint family has deep blue to purple flowers borne in tight, tiered spikes at the tips of branching 1½- to 3-foot stems. The foliage has a strong musty scent. This species is often crossed with *S. pratensis* to produce numerous outstanding garden hybrids listed as *S. × sylvestris.*

HOW TO GROW Plant meadow sage in well-drained sandy or loamy soils in full sun or light shade. It will get leggy and flop in too much shade. Overly rich soils also encourage flopping. Most species are tough and extremely drought-tolerant. Divide plants in spring or fall if they outgrow their position. Cut plants back to the ground in fall or early spring. Propagate by stem cuttings in early summer. Treat the less hardy species as annuals in colder zones and grow them from seed sown indoors or overwinter cuttings.

If grown in overly rich soil or too much shade, meadow sage tends to flop.

RELATED SPECIES Grown as an annual in the north, *Salvia farinacea*, mealy-cup sage, has open, loosely branching stems 2 to 4 feet tall and terminal spikes of violet-blue flowers held above the foliage. Zones 8 to 10. S. *leucantha*, velvet sage, is a shrubby species with felted leaves and 10-inch clusters of lavender flowers in late summer through autumn on 3- to 4-foot stems. Zones 8 to 10.

COMPANION PLANTS Sages add rich color and vertical form to borders with geraniums, sedums, irises, peonies, yuccas, yarrows (*Achillea*), daylilies (*Hemerocallis*), mums (*Chrysanthemum*), and grasses.

Silphium laciniatum
COMPASS PLANT

NATIVE HABITAT Moist to dry black-soil prairies and savannas from Ohio and Minnesota south to Alabama and Oklahoma

HARDINESS ZONES 4 to 8

Timid gardeners may never appreciate the commanding compass plant. Towering 4- to 8-foot stalks bear 5-inch flowers that resemble sunflowers. Huge 2-foot, deeply lobed leaves form decorative tufts 3 to 4 feet wide that are not easily ignored by even the most jaded gardener.

HOW TO GROW Plant in moist, well-drained, humus-rich soil. The small plants you set out will quickly grow to elephantine proportions, so leave plenty of room for them to spread. Established clumps are deep-rooted and impossible to divide.

RELATED SPECIES *Silphium compositum* has wavy 2-foot basal leaves like giant sea clams and slender, open spikes 4 to 6 feet tall with small yellow flowers. Zones 4 to 9. *S. integrifolium,* rosinweed, is an eye-catching species valued for its smaller size, 2 to 4 feet, and copious flowers in

Its large flowers and striking foliage make towering compass plant an ideal focal point among garden perennials or with wildflowers and grasses in a meadow.

domed clusters in high summer. Zones 3 to 9. *S. perfoliatum,* cup plant, has tall stems that pierce the leaf blades, forming a cup. In summer the 3-inch soft yellow flowers are carried on 3- to 8-foot stems in branched clusters just above the leaves. Zones 3 to 8. *S. terebinthinaceum,* prairie dock, has the most striking foliage in the genus. Heart-shaped 3-foot basal leaves form an open rosette below the 6- to 8-foot naked bloom stalks that bear branched clusters of 3-inch flowers. Zones 3 to 9.

COMPANION PLANTS Large flowers and striking foliage make compass plant an ideal specimen or focal point. Resist the temptation to relegate this beauty to the back of the border. Place plants where both the foliage and flowers show to best advantage among lower perennials with fine textures or in a meadow with wildflowers and grasses.

Solidago rugosa 'Fireworks'
'FIREWORKS' ROUGH-STEMMED GOLDENROD

NATIVE HABITAT Open woods, meadows, and old fields from Newfoundland and Michigan south to Florida and Texas

HARDINESS ZONES 4 to 9

'Fireworks' goldenrod is aptly named, for it lights up the late-season garden like a fiery explosion. Spectacular broad, open flower clusters with arching branches spread over erect, leafy stems 2 to 3 feet high.

HOW TO GROW Plant in average to rich, moist, well-drained soil in full sun or light shade. Plants grow from creeping rhizomes that form broad clumps, especially in rich soil. Pull up wanton runners to control the size of the clumps.

RELATED SPECIES *Solidago rigida*, stiff goldenrod, is a unique species with showy flattened flower clusters on erect stems 2 to 5 feet tall clothed in soft fuzzy leaves. Zones 3 to 9. *S. spathulata* is a creeping goldenrod with bright yellow 1- to 2-foot inflorescences atop stiff, horizontal branches with deep green paddle-shaped leaves. Zones 4 to 9. *S. speciosa,* showy goldenrod, has leafy, red-tinged stems crowned by dense branched spikes 1 to 3 feet tall in August and September. Zones 3 to 8. *S. juncea,* early goldenrod, is the first goldenrod to open, in late July or August, with branched terminal flower clusters over dense, clumping foliage rosettes. Zones 3 to 8.

COMPANION PLANTS Goldenrods are excellent for cottage gardens and meadows. For a border, choose a clump-forming species, or plant in a bottomless container to curb the spreading rhizomes. Purple and blue asters, salvias, and Russian sage (*Perovskia atriplicifolia*), along with orange sneezeweed (*Helenium*) and grasses make a stunning display.

Veronica peduncularis 'Georgia Blue'
'GEORGIA BLUE' SPEEDWELL

NATIVE HABITAT Open woods and meadows in eastern Europe and Turkey

HARDINESS ZONES 5 to 9

This fetching speedwell is a mat-forming profuse bloomer swamped with gentian-blue flowers from earliest spring through midsummer. The rounded, glossy green leaves turn purple to bronze in winter.

HOW TO GROW Plant speedwell in average to rich, moist but well-drained soil in full sun or light shade. Shear the plants after flowering to promote fresh, compact growth.

RELATED SPECIES *Veronica spicata,* spiked speedwell, has pointed pink, blue, or white flower clusters atop erect leafy 1- to 3-foot stems. Many named selections are available. Zones 3 to 8. *V. prostrata is* another blue-flowered creeper with a lovely yellow-leafed selection called 'Buttercup'. Zones 3 to 8. *V. repens* 'Sunshine' is another good yellow-leafed selection. Zones 7 to 9. *V. austriaca* subsp. *teucrium,* Hungarian speedwell, is a spreading species with bright blue erect flower spikes. Zones 3 to 8. *Veronicastrum virginicum,* Culver's root, is distinguished from *Veronica* by lance-shaped leaves borne in tiered whorls. It has erect creamy white candelabra spikes on 3- to 6-foot stems. *Veronicastrum virginicum* var. *sibericum* has erect to nodding blue spikes. Zones 4 to 8.

COMPANION PLANTS Place 'Georgia Blue' speedwell at the front of a border or along a walkway or wall for

To control the size of the clump, it's a good idea to pull up wanton runners of 'Fireworks' goldenrod.

Thriving with little care, North American native yucca is salt-, drought-, and shade-tolerant. After flowering, the main crown dies but basal offshoots keep the clump growing for years.

early color with daffodils, tulips, and other bulbs. The foliage is attractive all summer around yuccas, irises, and other spiky plants.

Yucca filamentosa
ADAM'S NEEDLE, YUCCA

NATIVE HABITAT Sand dunes, outcroppings, and pine barrens from Maryland to Georgia

HARDINESS ZONES 4 to 10

The stiff, swordlike leaves of yuccas instantly transport me to the desert. Nodding, creamy-white flowers with three petals and three petal-like sepals that form a bell dangle elegantly from erect, multibranched bloom stalks that rise 5 to 15 feet above the foliage.

HOW TO GROW Plant yuccas in average to rich, well-drained soil in full sun or light shade. Established plants are drought- and shade-tolerant and thrive for years with little care. After

flowering, the main crown dies but basal offshoots keep the clumps growing. Plants are salt-tolerant.

RELATED SPECIES *Y. flaccida* is similar to Adam's needle, but the leaves are thinner-textured, with drooping tips. Zones 4 to 9. *Y. rostrata* forms a nearly spherical rosette of narrow blue needles atop a short, woody trunk. Zones 5 to 10.

COMPANION PLANTS Yuccas bring a touch of the Southwest to our gardens. Choose them as accent plants in a border or use them massed on a bank in a seaside garden. Contrast is the key to showing off yuccas. Combine the stiff, upright foliage with mounding plants such as gauras, catmints (*Nepeta*), Mongolian aster (*Kalimeris pinnatifida*), sundrops (*Oenothera*), salvias, and creeping veronicas (*Veronica repens* and *V. austriaca* subsp. *teucrium*).

COMPANION SHRUBS FOR MOIST AREAS

PLANT	ZONES	BLOOM TIME	COLOR
Abelia × grandiflora Glossy abelia	5 to 9	Summer	Pink
Aesculus pavia Red buckeye	6 to 9	Spring	Red
Agarista populifolia Florida leucothoe	7 to 9	Spring	White
Camellia sasanqua, C. japonica Camellia	7 to 10	Fall/spring	White, pink, red
Caryopteris clandonensis Blue spirea	5 to 9	Late summer	Blue
Chionanthus retusus Chinese fringe tree	6 to 8	Spring	White
Clerodendrum trichotomum Glorybower	7 to 9	Summer	White
Cornus florida Flowering dogwood	5 to 8	Spring	White
Corylopsis spicata Winterhazel	5 to 8	Late winter	Yellow
Cotinus coggygria Smokebush	4 to 8	Summer	Pink
Cotoneaster salicifolius Cotoneaster	4 to 8	Late spring	White
Daphne odora Daphne	4 to 9	Winter	White, pink
Deutzia corymbosa Deutzia	4 to 8	Spring	White, pink
Edgeworthia chrysantha Paperbush	7 to 9	Winter	Yellow
Forsythia hybrids Forsythia	4 to 8	Late winter	Yellow
Hamamelis × intermedia Witch-hazel	5 to 8	Winter	Yellow, orange
Kolkwitzia amabilis Beautybush	4 to 8	Spring	Pink
Magnolia stellata Star magnolia	4 to 8	Early spring	White, pink
Loropetalum chinense Chinese fringe flower	7 to 9	Spring	White
Neviusia alabamensis Alabama snow wreath	5 to 8	Spring	White
Osmanthus fragrans Fragrant osmanthus	7 to 9	Autumn	White
Pieris japonica Lily-of-the-valley shrub	5 to 8	Late winter	White
Prunus mume Japanese apricot	6 to 9	Winter	Pink, white
Rhododendron Deciduous azalea	5 to 9	Spring	White, pink, yellow
Rhododendron Evergreen rhododendron	6 to 8	Summer	White, pink
Rosa glauca Rose	4 to 8	Spring/summer	Pink
Spiraea thunbergii 'Ogon' Spirea	4 to 8	Summer	White, pink
Stewartia malacodendron Silky camellia	5 to 8	Summer	White
Styrax americanus Snowbell	5 to 8	Spring	White
Syringa vulgaris Lilac	3 to 7	Spring	White, purple

Perennials for Wet Areas

Alchemilla mollis
LADY'S MANTLE

NATIVE HABITAT Wet meadows and streamsides in the eastern Carpathians, Turkey, and the Caucasus

HARDINESS ZONES 4 to 8

The frothy mounds of acid-yellow spring flowers make lady's mantle a standout in any garden situation. The broad clumps of soft, hairy, pleated foliage spread slowly outward from creeping rootstocks. Water forms silvery beads on the felted leaves. Visitors to English gardens fall under the spell of this plant, which does well in North American gardens, except those in the hot, humid South.

HOW TO GROW Plant lady's mantle in rich, moist soil in sun or partial shade. Plants prefer cool conditions and consistent moisture, so grow them in partial shade where summers are hot. Cut plants to the ground after flowering or if the foliage becomes brown or tattered. Clumps will quickly produce a new set of fresh, attractive leaves.

RELATED SPECIES *Alchemilla alpina*, mountain mantle, is a low, delicate plant to 8 inches high with deeply lobed starry leaves edged with silver hairs. It is extremely cold-hardy and intolerant of excessive heat. Zones 3 to 7. *A. erythropoda* is a miniature version of *A. mollis*, just 6 to 8 inches tall. *A. conjuncta* is similar but grows to 12 or more inches. Both thrive in moist, well-drained sites and are hardy in Zones 4 to 8.

An established clump of boltonia is quite drought-tolerant, but if the soil is consistently dry the plants will be stunted.

COMPANION PLANTS Place lady's mantle at the front of the perennial border or use it as an edging plant along a wall or walkway. It is perfect for a low damp spot or a moist border with cranesbills (*Geranium*), astilbes, and sedges.

Boltonia asteroides
BOLTONIA

NATIVE HABITAT Wet meadows, prairies, and marshes from New Jersey and North Dakota south to Florida and Texas

HARDINESS ZONES 3 to 9

Boltonia in bloom looks like snow in September. Upright stems 4 to 6 feet tall with blue-green willowlike foliage bear a profusion of dainty, 1-inch white asterlike flowers with

Requiring moist to wet soil, European tussock sedge thrives in standing water at the edge of a pond or as a container plant in a water garden.

yellow centers throughout late summer and autumn. Plants grow from stout crowns with long fibrous roots. 'Snowbank' is superior to the species in flower size and number.

HOW TO GROW Plant boltonias in moist to wet, humus-rich soil in full sun or light shade. Established plants are tolerant of drought, but if the soil is consistently dry the plants will be stunted. Clumps form tough woody bases as they age and may need division after five years or so to invigorate them.

COMPANION PLANTS Boltonias are perfect for borders as well as meadow gardens. If you have a wet area such as a ditch, boltonias will thrive there, beautifying an eyesore. Some good companions include joe-pye weed (*Eupatorium*), sunflowers (*Helianthus*), sneezeweed (*Helenium*), lobelias, ironweed (*Vernonia*), and monkshoods (*Aconitum*).

Carex elata 'Aurea'
EUROPEAN TUSSOCK SEDGE
NATIVE HABITAT Swamps, marshes, and riverbanks throughout Europe

HARDINESS ZONES 5 to 8

Tussock sedge is seldom seen in its native green-leafed form. It is the golden-variegated selection 'Aurea' that has endeared this plant to gardeners looking for a little drama. The huge foliage mounds to 3 feet tall and wide are striking when illuminated by the sun, or as a spot of light in the evening garden. Drooping flower clusters hang like catkins from wiry stems above the foliage.

HOW TO GROW Plant in consistently moist to wet, humus-rich soil in full sun or partial shade. Plants will grow in standing water at the edge of a natural pond or as containerized plants in a water garden. They tolerate considerable shade, but the foliage will be paler and the plants will flop.

Though native to wetlands in the Appalachian Mountains, pink turtleheads are quite adaptable to garden conditions, provided they are planted in evenly moist soil.

RELATED SPECIES *Carex pendula,* drooping sedge, is a dramatic, clumping plant with stiffly arching blades 2 to 3 feet tall in dense clumps. The stiff catkins dangle well above the foliage on 4- to 6-foot stems. Zones 5 to 9. *C. spissa,* San Diego sedge, has silver-blue leaves in gracefully arching clumps 2 to 5 feet tall. Zones 8 to 10.

COMPANION PLANTS Use tussock sedge as a specimen to draw your eye to a stunning combination of bold foliage plants or as a soft, fountainlike accent in a water garden. Good companions include cannas, elephant ears (*Colocasia*), callas (*Zantedeschia aethiopica*), turtleheads (*Chelone*), and ferns.

Chelone lyonii
PINK TURTLEHEAD
NATIVE HABITAT Wet ditches and meadows in the Appalachian Mountains from North Carolina to Tennessee

HARDINESS ZONES 3 to 8

Turtlehead takes its name from its unusual inflated tubular flower, which resembles the head of a turtle with its mouth agape. Bright rose-pink flowers are borne in late summer on sturdy, compact stems 1 to 3 feet tall. Deep green quilted leaves are arrayed in pairs along the stem. The dried seed heads are also attractive.

HOW TO GROW Though native to wetlands, turtleheads are quite adaptable to garden conditions. Plant them in rich, evenly moist soil in full sun or partial shade. In warmer zones, provide constant moisture and some shade. Divide overgrown clumps by pulling apart the fleshy-rooted crowns in spring or late fall after flowering. Different turtlehead species hybridize freely in the garden.

RELATED SPECIES *Chelone glabra,* white turtlehead, is a graceful upright to arching vase-shaped plant 3 to 5 feet tall with white flowers blushed with violet. The dark green leaves are lance-shaped. Zones 3 to 8. *C. obliqua*, red turtlehead, is a floriferous species with rose to pale pink flowers in axillary clusters along arching 2- to 3-foot stems. Leaves are narrower and have shorter stalks than those of the similar pink turtlehead. Zones 4 to 9.

COMPANION PLANTS In both formal and informal gardens, plant turtleheads with Japanese anemones (*Anemone × hybrida*), asters, goldenrods (*Solidago*), sunflowers (*Helianthus*), joe-pye weed (*Eupatorium*), and grasses. Plants are beautiful in drifts in meadow gardens or at the edge of a pond, where the flowers are reflected in the still water alongside sedges and ferns.

Eupatorium purpureum
SWEET JOE-PYE WEED
NATIVE HABITAT Low meadows, marshes, and seeps from New Hampshire and Iowa south to Georgia and Oklahoma

HARDINESS ZONES 3 to 8

A drift of sweet joe-pye weed looks like billowing pink cumulus clouds rising above the summer garden. Beautiful 3- to 6-foot clumps are crowned with domed to rounded clusters of pale red-violet, sweet-scented flowers. The foliage is vanilla-scented when bruised.

HOW TO GROW Plant joe-pye weed in moist to wet rich soil in full sun or light shade. Established plants are tough and need little attention. It takes two seasons for new plants to reach their prodigious mature size. Self-sown seedlings may be numerous.

RELATED SPECIES *Eupatorium purpureum* 'Atropurpureum' is a superb selection with compact 5- to 6-foot

When bruised, the foliage of sweet joe-pye weed gives off a vanilla scent.

deep purple stems, dark leaves, and soft raspberry-colored, sweet-scented flowers. *E. fistulosum*, joe-pye weed, is a giant species with 6- to 14-foot straight stems crowned by elongated domes of dusty-rose flowers in summer. Zones 4 to 9. *E. maculatum*, spotted joe-pye weed, is a relatively short species 4 to 6 feet tall with flattened clusters of rose-purple flowers. Zones 2 to 8. *Eupatorium coelestinum,* hardy ageratum, has sprawling stems 2 to 3 feet tall topped with fluffy clusters of powder-blue flowers in late summer and fall. Zones 4 to 10.

COMPANION PLANTS Joe-pye weed looks great anywhere. Place it at the rear of a border or in a meadow at the edge of the woods with bee balms (*Monarda*), marsh mallows (*Hibiscus moscheutos*), sneezeweed (*Helenium autumnale*), goldenrods (*Solidago*),

91

asters, and grasses. The seed heads are attractive in the winter laced with frost or snow.

Filipendula rubra
QUEEN-OF-THE-PRAIRIE, MEADOWSWEET

NATIVE HABITAT Low meadows, prairies, and ditches from New York and Wisconsin south to North Carolina and Kentucky; naturalized outside its range

HARDINESS ZONES 3 to 9

Queen-of-the-prairie waves its frothy hot-pink cotton-candy heads high above other plants for all to see. Rising above dramatic basal rosettes, the wiry 4- to 6-foot-tall bloom stalks are sparsely clothed with attractive maplelike leaves.

HOW TO GROW Plant frivolous queen-of-the-prairie in evenly moist to wet, humus-rich soil in full sun or light shade. If the soil is too dry, the leaves become tattered or crispy. Cut old leaves and stalks to the ground after

flowering and fresh foliage will emerge. Clumps spread rapidly by creeping stems and need frequent division to keep them from overrunning their neighbors. Powdery mildew may occur on plants grown in hot, dry gardens.

RELATED SPECIES *Filipendula purpurea,* Siberian meadowsweet, is a compact species 3 to 4 feet tall with deep rose-pink flowers and starry leaves. Zones 4 to 9. *F. ulmaria,* queen-of-the-meadow, has white to pale pink flowers on 2- to 4-foot stems. Zones 3 to 8.

COMPANION PLANTS Queen-of-the-prairie adds drama to formal borders and meadows. The plants grow lushest along a stream or at the edge of a pond where the fluffy heads are reflected in the water. Combine the flamboyant flowers with joe-pye weed (*Eupatorium*), ferns, and grasses.

Helenium autumnale
SNEEZEWEED, HELEN'S FLOWER

NATIVE HABITAT Low-lying woods, wet meadows, and prairies from Quebec and British Columbia south to Florida and Arizona

HARDINESS ZONES 3 to 8

Sneezeweed is a delicate yellow daisy that starts blooming in early autumn. Erect 3- to 5-foot leafy stems are topped by broad clusters of 2-inch yellow-orange, yellow-centered flowers. The lemon-scented flower heads will not make you sneeze, however, as the pollen is carried by insects, not the wind. The name sneezeweed was coined at a time when the powdered

Divide rapidly spreading queen-of-the-prairie frequently to keep it from overrunning its neighbors in the garden.

Give marsh mallows ample room when planting. The dramatic perennials grow as large as shrubs and resent transplanting.

roots of the plant were used to make snuff.

HOW TO GROW Plant sneezeweed in evenly moist to wet humus-rich soil in full sun or light shade. Some cultivars are naturally compact and self-supporting, while others need staking. To keep the clumps vigorous, divide them every three to four years, replanting into enriched soil.

RELATED SPECIES *Helenium flexuosum,* purple-headed sneezeweed, has compact 3-foot leafy stems and broad, domed clusters of flowers with drooping yellow rays and brownish purple spherical centers. Zones 5 to 9. *H. hoopesii,* orange sneezeweed, resembles a coneflower with ragged drooping yellow-orange rays. Plants need good drainage. Zones 3 to 8.

COMPANION PLANTS Sneezeweed adds an indispensable spot of bright

autumn color to borders and meadows. Combine it with irises, garden phlox, marsh mallows (*Hibiscus moscheutos*), asters, joe-pye weed (*Eupatorium*), goldenrods (*Solidago*), ironweed (*Vernonia*), ferns, and grasses.

Hibiscus moscheutos
MARSH MALLOW, ROSE MALLOW

NATIVE HABITAT Wet meadows, low-lying woods, marshes, and ditches from Maryland and Ohio south to Indiana and Texas

HARDINESS ZONES 4 (with protection) to 10

Marsh mallows are dramatic perennials that grow as large as shrubs, with 6- to 8-inch red-centered white flowers crowding the upper ends of the stems. Individual flowers last only one day, opening in succession over three to six weeks. The deeply lobed leaves resemble those of maples. The woody seed capsules are quite attractive in fall and winter.

HOW TO GROW Plant marsh mallows in evenly moist, humus-rich soil in full sun or light shade. Leave at least 3 feet between the plants to allow for their eventual spread, since once established, they do not transplant well. Cultivars do not come true from seed, but the seedlings, though not identical to their parents, are attractive in their own right. Japanese beetles may munch on the leaves. Pick them off and drop them in a pail of soapy water.

RELATED SPECIES *Hibiscus moscheutos* subsp. *palustris,* marsh mallow, is a coastal plant with three-lobed leaves and rose-pink or white flowers without an eye. Many hybrids have been made combining the compact growth and huge 8- to 10-inch flowers in a range of colors from pure white to pink, rose, and bright red. Zones 4 to 9. *H. coccineus,* scarlet rose mallow, is a stately giant 5 to 10 feet tall with broad, deeply incised palmately lobed leaves and stunning 6-inch saucer-shaped scarlet flowers. Zones 7 to 10. *Kosteletzkya virginica,* seaside mallow, is a refined hibiscus relative with 1- to 4-foot stalks bearing clusters of 3-inch, clear deep pink flowers. Zones 6 to 9.

COMPANION PLANTS Marsh mallows are dramatic accent plants that add a bold stroke of color to a border with airy summer perennials and grasses. In meadow or waterside gardens, combine them with ferns, astilbes, and ornamental grasses.

Cardinal flowers bloom for a long period; the tops of the spikes may be in full flower while the lower portions already carry ripened seed.

Lobelia cardinalis
CARDINAL FLOWER
NATIVE HABITAT Low meadows, wet woods, and stream banks from New Brunswick and Minnesota south to Florida and the Gulf states

HARDINESS ZONES 2 to 9

The deep blood-red spires of cardinal flower make a summer border as hot as the summer air. Dense spikes of flaming flowers crown leafy stems 2 to 4 feet tall. Each $1\frac{1}{2}$-inch flower looks like a bird rising in flight. Plants bloom for a long period, and the tops of the spikes can be in full flower while the lower portions may already carry ripened seed.

HOW TO GROW Plant in rich, constantly moist soil in full sun to partial shade. Plants resent mulch resting on their evergreen winter rosettes and may rot if not uncovered in early spring. They are often short-lived and should be divided every two to three

The colorful mounds of North American native bee balm attract the attention of hummingbirds and other nectar lovers, such as bumblebees.

years to stay vigorous. Lift clumps in early fall and remove the new rosettes from the old rootstocks. Replant immediately in enriched soil. Self-sown seedlings may be plentiful on bare soil.

RELATED SPECIES *Lobelia × gerardii,* purple lobelia, is a showy 3- to 4-foot royal-purple-flowered hybrid. Zones 4 to 8. *L. siphilitica,* great blue lobelia, has deep blue "buck-toothed" flowers in midsummer on 2- to 3-foot leafy stalks. This species is important in hybridization. Zones 3 to 8. *L. × speciosa* is a variable group of sturdy, floriferous hybrids that have revolutionized lobelia as a border plant. Zones 5 (3 with protection) to 9.

COMPANION PLANTS Cardinal flowers add colorful exclamation points to the late-summer garden. Combine the brazen flowers with garden phlox, cannas, hibiscus, daylilies (*Hemerocallis*),

and ornamental grasses. In a moist meadow or water garden, plant them with astilbes, turtleheads (*Chelone*), sneezeweed (*Helenium*), ironweed (*Vernonia*), ferns, and sedges.

Monarda didyma
BEE BALM, OSWEGO TEA
NATIVE HABITAT Moist open woods, shaded roadsides, and clearings from Maine and Michigan south to New Jersey and Ohio; in the mountains to Georgia

HARDINESS ZONES 3 to 8

The brilliant scarlet spherical heads of bee balm shout for attention in the high summer garden. The 1-inch tubular flowers have distinctive protruding upper lips that arch over the smaller lower ones. Like other mints, they grow from fast-creeping runners with fibrous roots, have square stems (2 to 4 feet tall), and aromatic leaves. Tea

95

aficionados will recognize the pungent aroma of bee balm, which is similar to bergamot orange (*Citrus bergamia*), used in making Earl Grey tea.

HOW TO GROW Plant bee balm in humus-rich, evenly moist soils in full sun or partial shade. Plants spread rapidly outward in a circle and die out in the center. Lift and divide the entire clump every two to three years. Replant vigorous portions into enriched soil. Never allow the plants to dry out, as wilted leaves are quickly infested with powdery mildew. All cultivars show some degree of susceptibility to the disease, which causes white blotches on the leaves. Resistance seems as dependent on region and cultural conditions as it does on cultivar selection.

RELATED SPECIES Many garden selections have been named, some of which may be hybrids with bergamot (*M. fistulosa*).

COMPANION PLANTS The colorful mounds of bee balm attract the attention of hummingbirds as well as gardeners. In borders combine them with cranesbills (*Geranium*), garden phlox, shasta daisies (*Chrysanthemum* × *superbum*), dahlias, joe-pye weed (*Eupatorium*), and grasses. In a meadow or along a stream plant them with queen-of-the-prairie (*Filipendula rubra*), turtleheads (*Chelone*), sneezeweed (*Helenium*), and ferns.

Osmunda regalis var. *spectabilis*
ROYAL FERN, FLOWERING FERN
NATIVE HABITAT Wet woods, swamps, and seepage slopes from Newfoundland and Saskatchewan south to tropical America

HARDINESS ZONES 3 to 10

Plant moisture-loving royal fern along streams and pond margins, in wet swales, and in water gardens.

The tall, dissected sea-green fronds of royal fern have narrow linear segments like a meadow rue. They are crowned with beaded clusters of spore-producing sori. The odd placement of the sori at the tip of the fronds, where they look like a cluster of flower buds, gave rise to the common name flowering fern. Plants produce whorls of fronds 3 to 6 feet tall that emerge tinted pink in spring from thick, fibrous rhizomes.

HOW TO GROW Plant royal ferns in consistently moist to wet, humus-rich to mucky acidic soil in sun or shade. They will grow in standing water or containerized in a water garden. Plants will slowly decline if the soil is too dry. Royal fern is slow to establish and resents disturbance. Once mature, the huge plants are striking.

Growing from dense, tufted, multicrowned clumps, long-lived Stokes' aster is easily divided in spring or fall. Above is a pink cultivar.

RELATED SPECIES *Osmunda regalis* var. *regalis* is native to Europe and may grow 8 feet tall or more. Zones 4 to 8. *O. cinnamomea*, cinnamon fern, has bright green upright, less dissected fronds that reach 2 to 5 feet tall. New fronds emerge wrapped in tawny wool. Zones 2 to 10.

COMPANION PLANTS Use royal ferns along streams and pond margins, in wet swales, and in water gardens. They grow comfortably with any plant that thrives on moisture. Plant them with cannas, elephant ears (*Colocasia*), hibiscus, and sedges.

Stokesia laevis
STOKES' ASTER
NATIVE HABITAT Low wet pine woods, bottomlands, and ditches from North Carolina to Florida and Louisiana

HARDINESS ZONES 5 to 9

Stokes' aster adds a touch of blue to the midsummer garden as the catmints (*Nepeta*) are fading and before the asters hold court. Branched flower stalks bearing a gaggle of flat, ragged flowers rise 1 to 2 feet from the center of a clump of glossy, linear leaves, each with a conspicuous white midvein.

HOW TO GROW Plant Stoke's asters in rich, moist to wet soil in full sun or light shade. They are easy-to-grow, long-lived perennials that thrive under average garden conditions despite their wet natural habitats. They form dense, tufted multicrowned clumps that are easily divided in spring or fall. Plants will rebloom if deadheaded.

COMPANION PLANTS Contrast the bold, frilly flowers of long-blooming

Tall and striking, meadow rue easily dominates a border. It fits equally well into a meadow or an exuberant formal garden.

Stokes' asters with small flowers and fine-textured foliage such as phlox, yarrows (*Achillea*), and ornamental grasses. They do well in partial shade with columbines (*Aquilegia*), sedges, ferns, and hostas.

Thalictrum rochebrunianum
MEADOW RUE

NATIVE HABITAT Seepage slopes and wet meadows in Japan

HARDINESS ZONES 3 to 8

Some tall plants beg to be sited at the front of the border, and meadow rue is one of them. In late summer, this diaphanous beauty creates a lavender veil through which the brilliant colors of the approaching autumn seem to glow. The showy flowers have persistent colorful sepals and bright yellow stamens. The gray-green dissected foliage consists of many small scalloped leaflets.

HOW TO GROW Meadow rues are easy to grow in moist to wet, humus-rich soil in full sun or light shade. They form dense clumps with age that bear many bloom stalks. Plants seldom need division, but they can be lifted in fall and pulled apart to increase the stock.

RELATED SPECIES *Thalictrum aquilegiifolium,* columbine meadow rue, forms a frothy lavender or white haze in early summer. The only drawback to this attractive species is its short bloom season. Zones 4 to 8. *T. flavum* subsp. *glaucum,* yellow meadow rue, has blue broccoli-like buds that open to soft sulfur clouds on 3- to 5-foot stems. Yellow meadow rue is an open, lacy-crowned plant with large, dissected foliage. Stake the plants early, as they tend to flop as soon as the flowers open. Zones 4 to 8. *T. lucidum* is perhaps the most distinctive meadow rue, with erect, conical clusters of soft yellow flowers atop self-supporting 4- to 5-foot stems. The deep green leaves with linear, unlobed leaflets are a unique aspect of this species. Zones 4 to 8. *T. delavayi* 'Hewlett's Double' wins the prize for best flower display, with drooping sprays of double lavender flowers late in the season over very finely textured foliage. Zones 4 to 8.

COMPANION PLANTS A well-grown meadow rue can easily dominate a border. A single stately clump makes a dramatic focal point, and the plants fit comfortably into meadows and exuberant formal gardens. Plant them with garden phlox, daylilies (*Hemerocallis*), masterworts (*Astrantia*), sneezeweed (*Helenium*), marsh mallows (*Hibiscus moscheutos*), and grasses.

Thelypteris kunthii
SOUTHERN MAIDEN FERN, RIVER FERN

NATIVE HABITAT Wet woods, savannas, and roadsides from South Carolina to Texas and Arkansas

HARDINESS ZONES 7 to 10

Southern maiden fern forms a beautiful tangle of bright sea-green fronds 2 to 4 feet tall from a creeping, branching rhizome. Plants form broad clumps that will fill any available space. In the South, the once-divided deciduous fronds remain green well into autumn, turning tawny with the first frost.

HOW TO GROW Plant southern maiden fern in moist to wet, acidic, average to humus-rich soil in sun or shade. Plants need shade where the soil is not consistently moist. They are fast-growing and may become weedy, especially in moist, fertile soil. Divide overgrown clumps in spring or fall.

RELATED SPECIES *Thelypteris noveboracensis*, New York fern, has tight mats of upright 1- to 2-foot, bright green fronds from fast-creeping rhizomes. Fronds turn golden yellow to straw-colored in autumn. Zones 3 to 8. *T. palustris,* marsh fern, produces wiry, bright green deciduous fronds 1 to 3 feet tall that stand in a line along the fast-creeping rhizome. Zones 2 to 9.

COMPANION PLANTS The soft restful fronds of southern maiden fern turn a garden into a cool oasis. Use them with large perennials such as joe-pye weed (*Eupatorium*), asters, irises, and grasses or in mass plantings with shrubs. They thrive along streams and at the edges of ponds, growing equally well in shaded gardens with hostas, ligularias, and sedges.

Vernonia altissima (*V. gigantea*)
TALL IRONWEED

NATIVE HABITAT Wet meadows and prairies, wetland edges, pond margins, and ditches from New York, Michigan, and Nebraska south to Georgia and Louisiana

HARDINESS ZONES 4 to 8

Tall, violet-flowered ironweed is the perfect antidote to the ubiquitous yellows of late summer. This gigantic species has stems 4 to 10 feet tall topped with dense, broad, flattened clusters of violet flowers in late summer and autumn. The stiff stems are clothed in deep green, broadly lance-shaped leaves. Presumably it's the rust-red hairs prominent in the spent flower heads and on the fruits that give ironweed its common name. Plants grow from woody, fibrous-rooted crowns.

HOW TO GROW Plant ironweed in rich, evenly moist to wet soil in full sun or light shade. Plants are easy to grow and thrive in most garden situations. Mature clumps are very large but seldom need division. If the clumps are too congested, thin the stems in late spring. Self-sown seedlings will appear. Leafminers may make pale tunnels in the leaves but do not harm the plants.

RELATED SPECIES *Vernonia fasciculata,* fascicled ironweed, is a compact, upright species 3 to 4 feet tall with toothed foliage and bowlike clusters of red-violet flowers in late summer. Zones 3 to 8. *V. lettermanii,* dwarf ironweed, has needlelike leaves on 2- to 3-foot stems and clustered violet flowers. Zones 4 to 9.

COMPANION PLANTS Ironweed provides a bold, colorful mass of flowers at the back of a herbaceous border or along the edge of a pond. Plant it with cannas, salvias, hibiscus, phlox, lobelias, joe-pye weed (*Eupatorium*), turtleheads (*Chelone*), asters, goldenrods (*Solidago*), ferns, and grasses.

Thriving in most garden situations, the stems of fall-flowering tall ironweed may reach 10 feet.

COMPANION SHRUBS FOR WET AREAS

PLANT	ZONES	BLOOM TIME	COLOR
Aronia species Chokeberry	4 to 9	Spring	White
Baccharis halimifolia Groundsel bush	5 to 9	Summer	White
Callicarpa americana Beautyberry	5 to 8	Summer	Lavender
Calycanthus floridus Carolina sweet shrub	4 to 9	Spring/summer	Red
Cephalanthus occidentalis Button bush	4 to 9	Summer	White
Chimonanthus praecox Wintersweet	6 to 9	Winter	Yellow
Clethra alnifolia Summersweet	4 to 9	Summer	White
Cornus sericea Red osier dogwood	2 to 8	Summer	White
Cyrilla racemiflora Titi	6 to 11	Summer	White
Gordonia lasianthus Gordonia	8 to 11	Summer	White
Hydrangea macrophylla Big-leaf hydrangea	6 to 9	Summer	Pink, blue
Hypericum prolificum Shrubby St. Johnswort	4 to 9	Late spring/summer	Yellow
Ilex glabra Inkberry holly	4 to 9	Summer	Green
Ilex verticillata Winterberry holly	3 to 8	Summer	White
Illicium floridanum Florida star anise	6 to 9	Spring	Red
Itea virginica Virginia sweetspire	5 to 9	Summer	White
Leucothoe racemosa Sweetbells	5 to 9	Spring/summer	White
Lindera benzoin Spicebush	5 to 8	Early spring	Yellow
Magnolia virginiana Sweetbay magnolia	5 to 9	Late spring/summer	White
Myrica cerifera Southern Waxmyrtle	7 to 10	Spring	Green
Myrica pensylvanica Bayberry	4 to 8	Spring	Green
Osmanthus americanus Devilwood	6 to 10	Spring	Green
Physocarpus opulifolius Ninebark	2 to 8	Summer	White
Rhododendron atlanticum Coast azalea	5 to 8	Spring	White
Rhododendron viscosum Swamp azalea	4 to 9	Summer	White
Salix 'Flame' Flame willow	3 to 9	Winter	Red
Sambucus canadensis Elderberry	3 to 9	Summer	White
Viburnum dentatum Arrowwood	3 to 8	Spring/summer	White
Viburnum nudum Smooth witherod	5 to 9	Summer	White
Viburnum trilobum American highbush cranberry	2 to 8	Late spring	White
Xanthorhiza simplicissima Shrub yellowroot	4 to 9	Early spring	Brown
Zenobia pulverulenta Dusty zenobia	5 to 9	Late spring	White

USDA Hardiness Zones

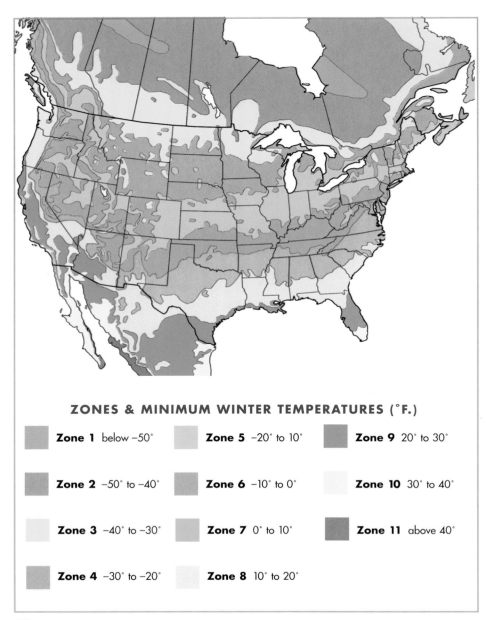

ZONES & MINIMUM WINTER TEMPERATURES (°F.)

Zone 1 below −50°

Zone 2 −50° to −40°

Zone 3 −40° to −30°

Zone 4 −30° to −20°

Zone 5 −20° to 10°

Zone 6 −10° to 0°

Zone 7 0° to 10°

Zone 8 10° to 20°

Zone 9 20° to 30°

Zone 10 30° to 40°

Zone 11 above 40°

For More Information

HERBACEOUS PERENNIAL PLANTS
Allan Armitage
Varsity Press, Athens, GA
1989

PERENNIAL COMBINATIONS
C. Colston Burrell
Rodale Press, 1999

PERENNIALS FOR TODAY'S GARDENS
C. Colston Burrell
Meredith Books, 2000

A GARDENER'S ENCYCLOPEDIA OF WILDFLOWERS
C. Colston Burrell
Rodale Press, 1997

THE GREEN TAPESTRY
Beth Chatto
Collier Books, 1988

THE DAMP GARDEN
Beth Chatto
J.N. Dent and Sons, Ltd.
London, 1982

THE DRY GARDEN
Beth Chatto
J.N. Dent and Sons, Ltd.
London, 1978

THE COLOR ENCYCLOPEDIA OF ORNAMENTAL GRASSES
Rick Darke
Timber Press, 1999

THE WELL-TENDED PERENNIAL GARDEN
Tracy DiSabato-Aust
Timber Press, 1998

THE NATURAL GARDEN
Ken Druse
C.N. Potter, 1989

DREAM PLANTS FOR THE NATURAL GARDEN
Henk Gerritsen and
Piet Oudolf
Timber Press, 2000

DESIGNING WITH PERENNIALS
Pamela J. Harper
Macmillan, 1991

COLOR ECHOES
Pamela J. Harper
Macmillan, 1994

THE GARDEN IN AUTUMN
Allen Lacy
Atlantic Monthly Press
1990

GARDEN FLOWERS
Christopher Lloyd
Cassell & Company
London, 2000

THE AMERICAN MIXED BORDER
Ann Lovejoy
Macmillan, 1993

FURTHER ALONG THE GARDEN PATH
Ann Lovejoy
Macmillan, 1995

FERNS FOR AMERICAN GARDENS
John Mickel
Macmillan, 1994

WILDFLOWER PERENNIALS FOR YOUR GARDEN
Bebe Miles
Hawthorne Books, 1976

RODALE'S ILLUSTRATED ENCYCLOPEDIA OF PERENNIALS
Ellen Phillips and
C. Colston Burrell
Rodale Press, 1993

PERENNIALS (TWO VOLUMES)
Roger Phillips and
Martin Rix
Random House, 1991

THE UNDAUNTED GARDEN
Lauren Springer
Fulcrum Publishing, 1994

PERENNIAL GARDEN PLANTS
Graham Stuart Thomas
Timber Press, 1990

Plant Sources

ARROWHEAD ALPINES
1310 North Gregory Road
Fowlerville, MI 48836
517-223-3581
www.arrowhead-alpines.com

CANYON CREEK NURSERY
3527 Dry Creek Road
Oroville, CA 95965
530-533-2166
www.canyoncreeknursery.com

COLLECTOR'S NURSERY
16804 NE 102nd Street
Battleground, WA 98604
360-574-3832
www.collectorsnursery.com

DIGGING DOG NURSERY
P.O. Box 471
Albion, CA 95410
707-937-1130
www.diggingdog.com

FANCY FRONDS
P.O. Box 1090
Gold Bar, WA 98251
360-793-1472
www.fancyfronds.com

FAIRWEATHER GARDENS
P.O. Box 330
Greenwich, NJ 08323
856-451-6261
www.fairweathergardens.com

FOREST FARM
990 Tetherow Road
Williams, OR 97544
541-846-7269
www.forestfarm.com

HERONSWOOD NURSERY
7530 NE 288th Street
Kingston, WA 98346
360-297-4172
www.heronswood.com

HIGH COUNTRY GARDENS
2902 Rufina Street
Santa Fe, NM 87507
800-925-9387
www.highcountrygardens.com

JOY CREEK NURSERY
20300 NW Watson Road
Scappoose, OR 97056
503-543-7474
www.joycreek.com

NATIVE GARDENS
5737 Fisher Lane
Greenback, TN 37742
865-856-0220
www.native-gardens.com

NICHE GARDENS
1111 Dawson Road
Chapel Hill, NC 27516
919-967-0078
www.nichegardens.com

PLANT DELIGHTS NURSERY
9241 Sauls Road
Raleigh, NC 27603
919-772-4794
www.plantdelights.com

PRAIRIE NURSERY
P.O. Box 306
Westfield, WI 53964
800-476-9453
www.prairienursery.com

PRIMROSE PATH
921 Scottdale-Dason Road
Scottdale, PA 15683
724-887-6756
www.theprimrosepath.com

ROSLYN NURSERY
211 Burrs Lane
Dix Hills, NY 11746
631-643-9347
www.roslynnursery.com

RUSSELL GRAHAM PURVEYOR OF PLANTS
4030 Eagle Crest Road, NW
Salem, OR 97304
503-362-1135

SENECA HILL PERENNIALS
3712 County Route 57
Oswego, NY 13126
315-342-5915
www.senecahill.com

SINGING SPRINGS NURSERY
8802 Wilkerson Road
Cedar Grove, NC 27231-9324
919-732-9403

SISKIYOU RARE PLANT NURSERY
2825 Cummings Road
Medford, OR 97501
541-772-6846
www.srpn.net

SUNLIGHT GARDENS
174 Golden Lane
Andersonville, TN 37705
800-272-7396
www.sunlightgardens.com

WE-DU NURSERIES
2055 Polly Spout Road
Marion, NC 28752
828-738-8300
www.we-du.com

WILD EARTH NATIVE PLANT NURSERY
49 Mead Avenue
Freehold, NJ 07728
732-308-9777

WOODLANDER'S INC.
1128 Colleton Avenue
Aiken, SC 29801
803-648-7522

Credits

C. COLSTON BURRELL is a garden designer, award-winning author, photographer, naturalist, and teacher. A certified chlorophyll addict, Burrell is an avid and lifelong plantsman and gardener. He is currently designing and planting a ten-acre garden of natives and the best plants of the global garden in the Blue Ridge Mountains near Charlottesville, Virginia. He is principal of Native Landscape Design and Restoration, a firm that specializes in blending nature and culture through artistic design. Burrell is the author of several books, including *Perennials for Today's Gardens, Perennial Combinations* (a best-selling Garden Book Club title), and *A Gardener's Encyclopedia of Wildflowers,* which won a 1998 American Horticultural Society Book Award. Burrell is a contributing editor to *Horticulture* magazine and also writes regularly for *Landscape Architecture, Fine Gardening,* and *American Gardener.* He is a frequent contributor to Brooklyn Botanic Garden publications. He edited the BBG handbooks *Woodland Gardens, The Natural Water Garden, Wildflower Gardens,* and *The Shady Border,* and, most recently, was a co-author of the BBG handbook *Summer-Blooming Bulbs.*

Burrell lectures internationally on garden design, plants, and ecology. He has worked as curator at the U.S. National Arboretum and the Minnesota Landscape Arboretum. His devotion to studying native plants in the wild and in gardens led to undergraduate degrees in botany and horticulture. He also holds an M.S. in horticulture and has integrated his interests in botany, horticulture, ecology, and design with a Master of Landscape Architecture degree from the University of Minnesota.

PHOTOS
ALAN & LINDA DETRICK cover, pages 6, 32 inset, 43, 45, 64, 67, 72, 73, 85, 94
DEREK FELL pages 1, 8, 18, 59, 66
DAVID CAVAGNARO pages 4, 7 top and bottom, 9, 11, 12, 14, 16, 20, 21 bottom, 24, 27 top and bottom, 29, 31, 32 top, 34, 36, 37, 38, 39, 40, 44, 47, 48, 49, 50, 53, 55, 56, 60, 63, 65, 68, 71 top and bottom, 75, 76, 77, 78, 79, 81, 83, 84, 88, 90, 91, 92, 93, 95, 97
C. COLSTON BURRELL pages 10, 13, 21 top, 41, 51, 52, 61, 69, 82, 89, 96, 100
BETH CHATTO page 22
NEIL SODERSTROM pages 26 top and bottom, 86
JERRY PAVIA pages 54, 58, 62, 70, 74
CHRISTINE DOUGLAS page 98

Index

BROOKLYN BOTANIC GARDEN

MICHAEL FUSCO

World renowned for pioneering gardening information, Brooklyn Botanic Garden's 21st-Century Gardening Series of award-winning guides provides spectacularly photographed, compact, practical advice for gardeners in every region of North America.

To order other fine titles published by BBG, call 718-623-7286, or shop in our online store at www.bbg.org/gardenemporium. For more information on Brooklyn Botanic Garden, including an online tour, visit www.bbg.org or call 718-623-7200.

MORE BOOKS ON GARDENING WITH PERENNIALS

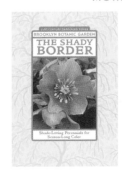